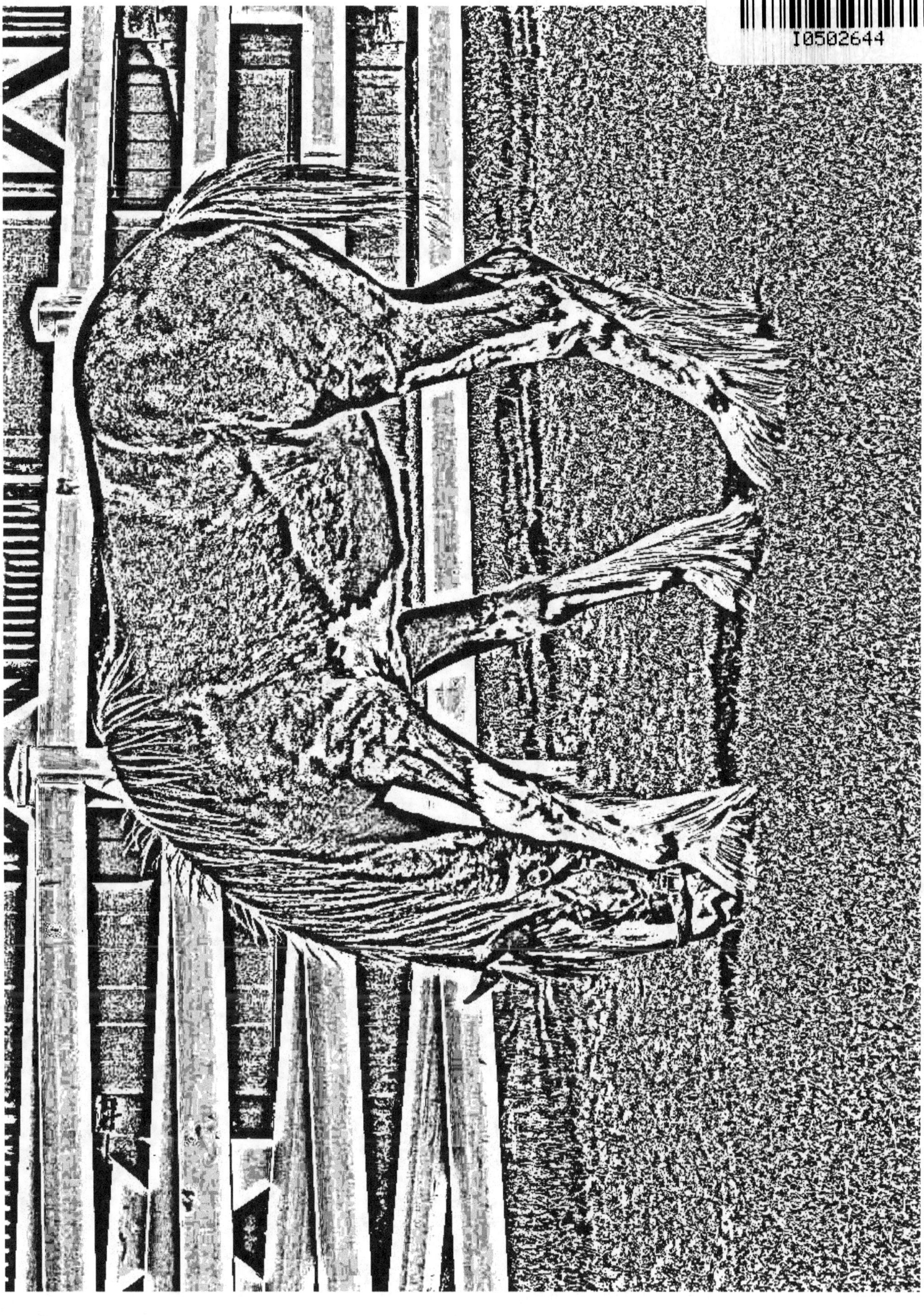

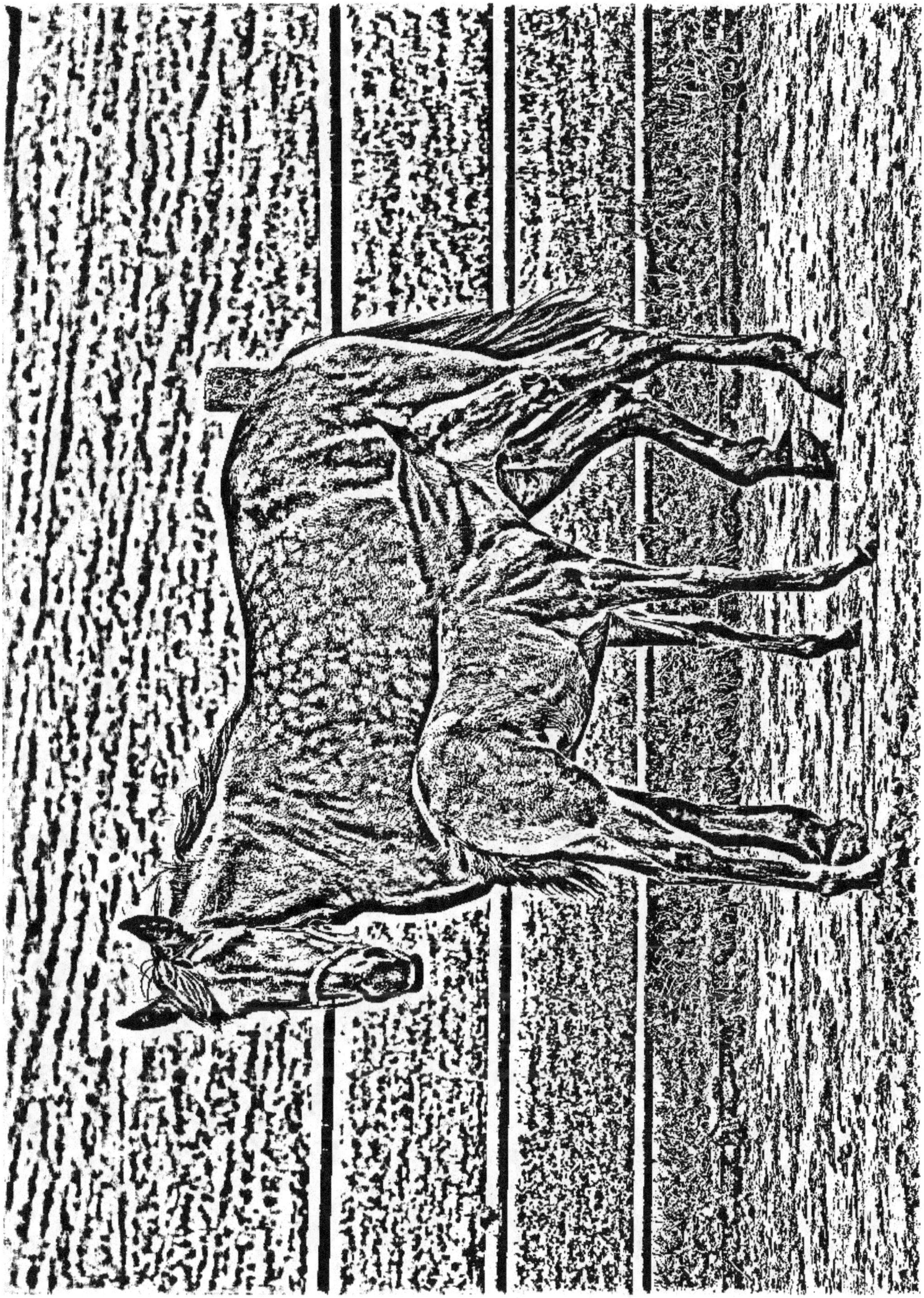

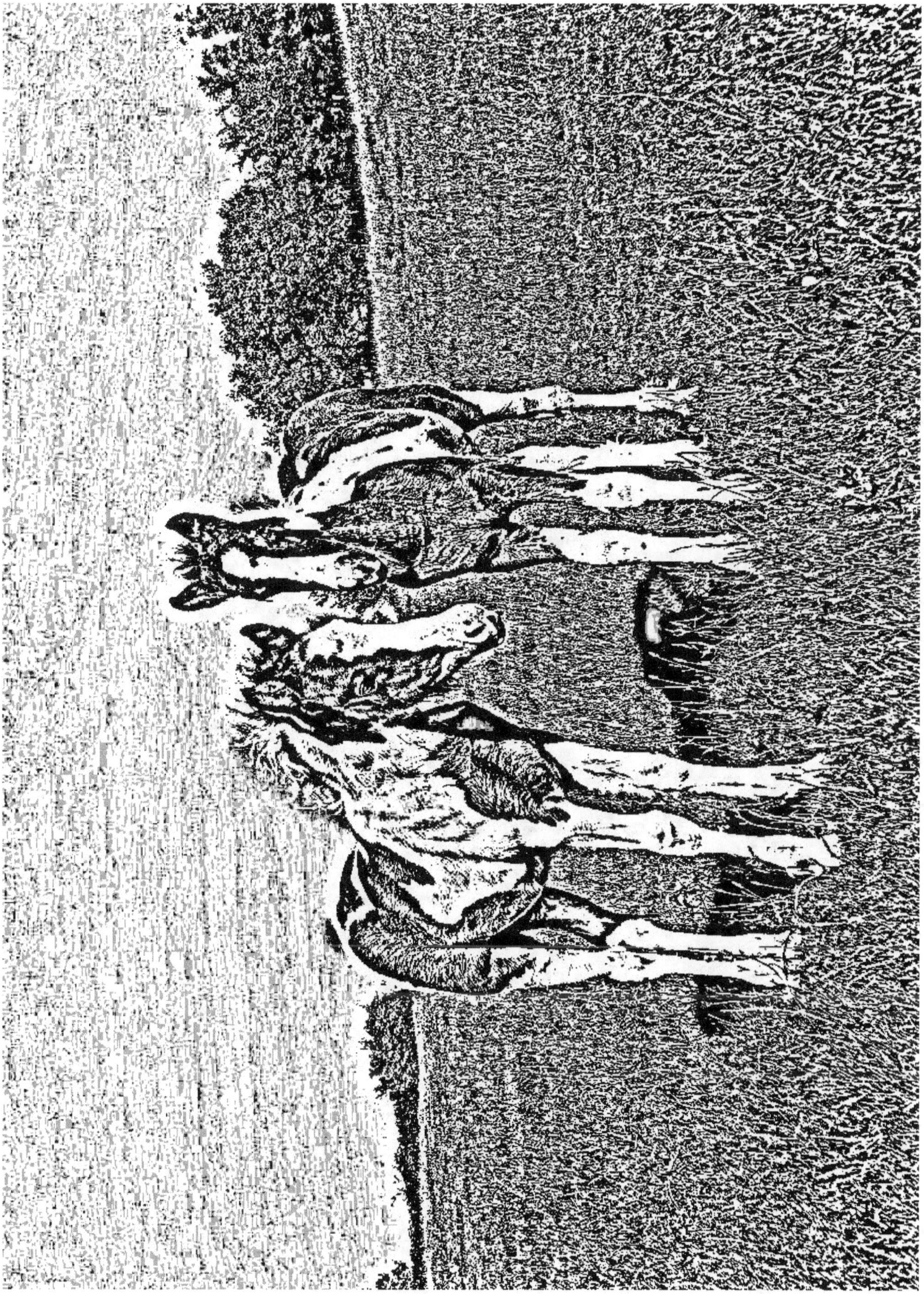

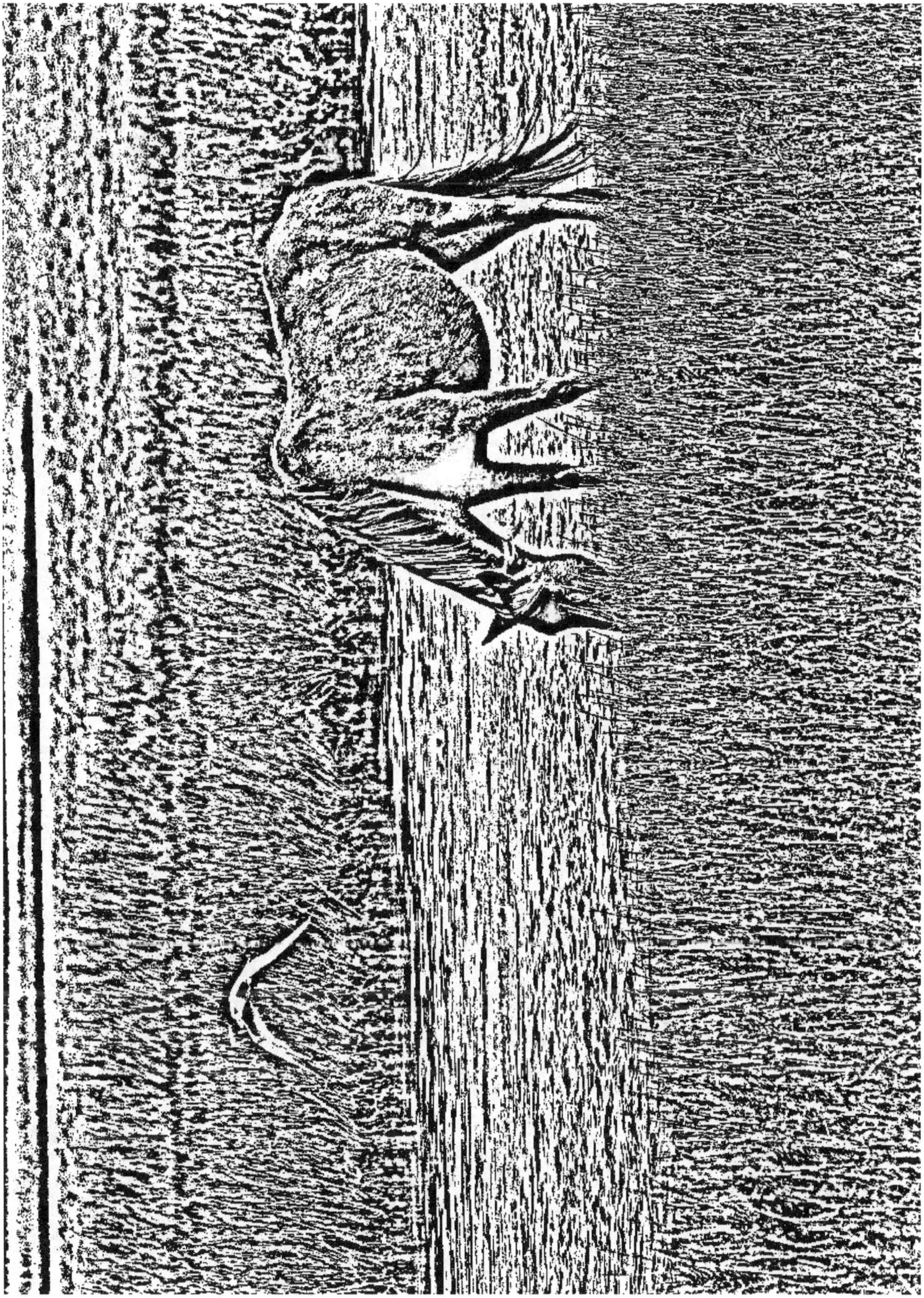

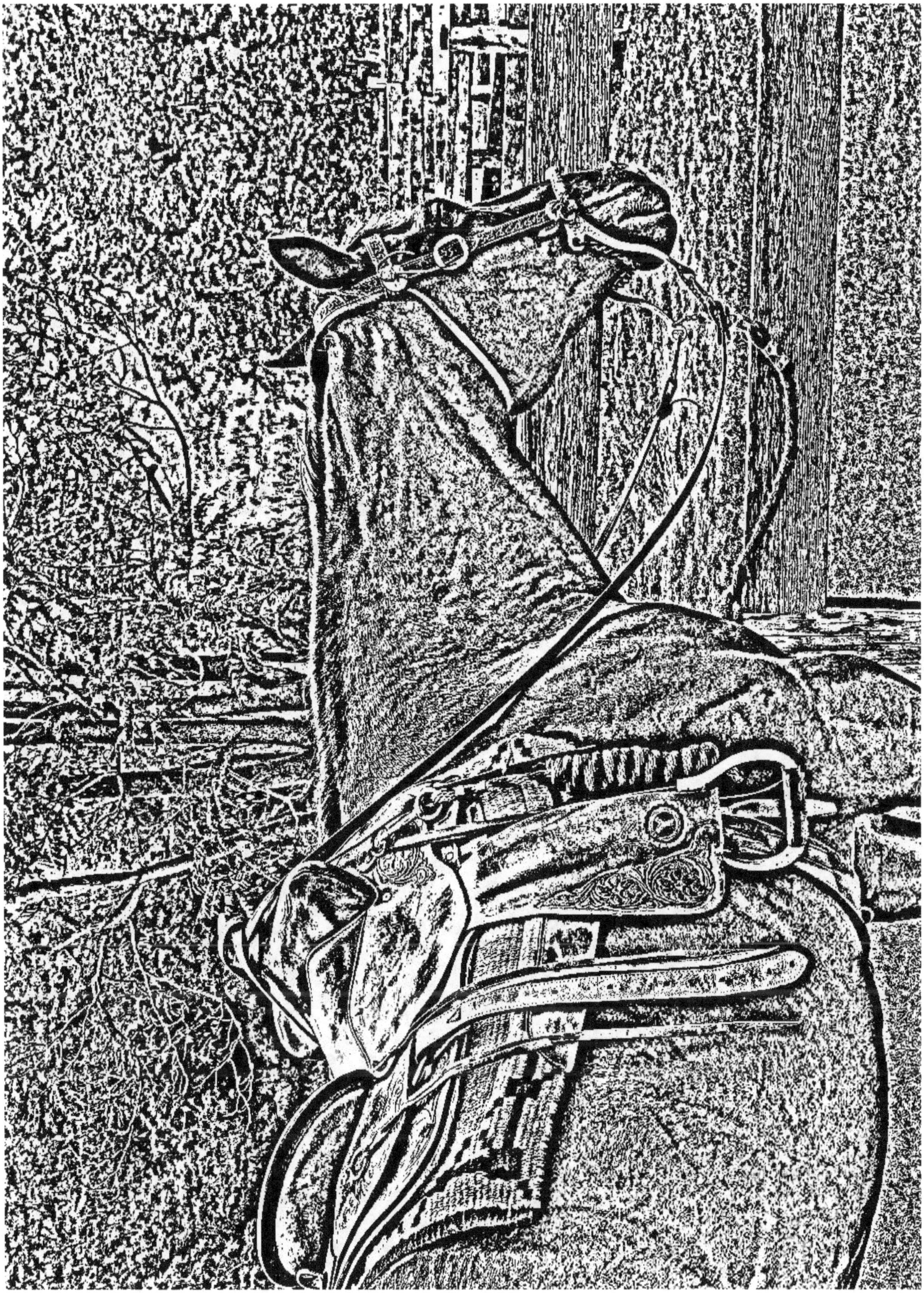

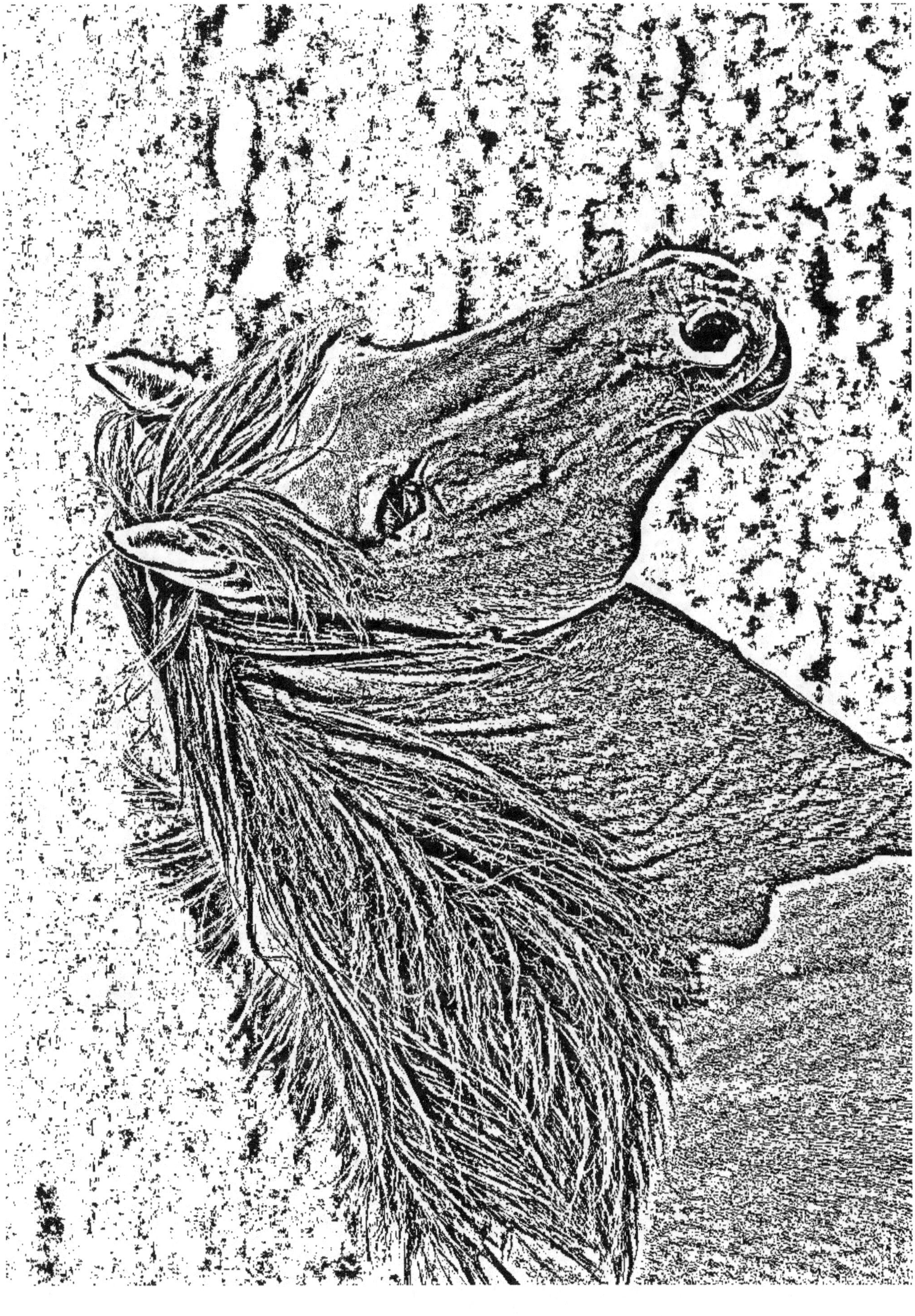

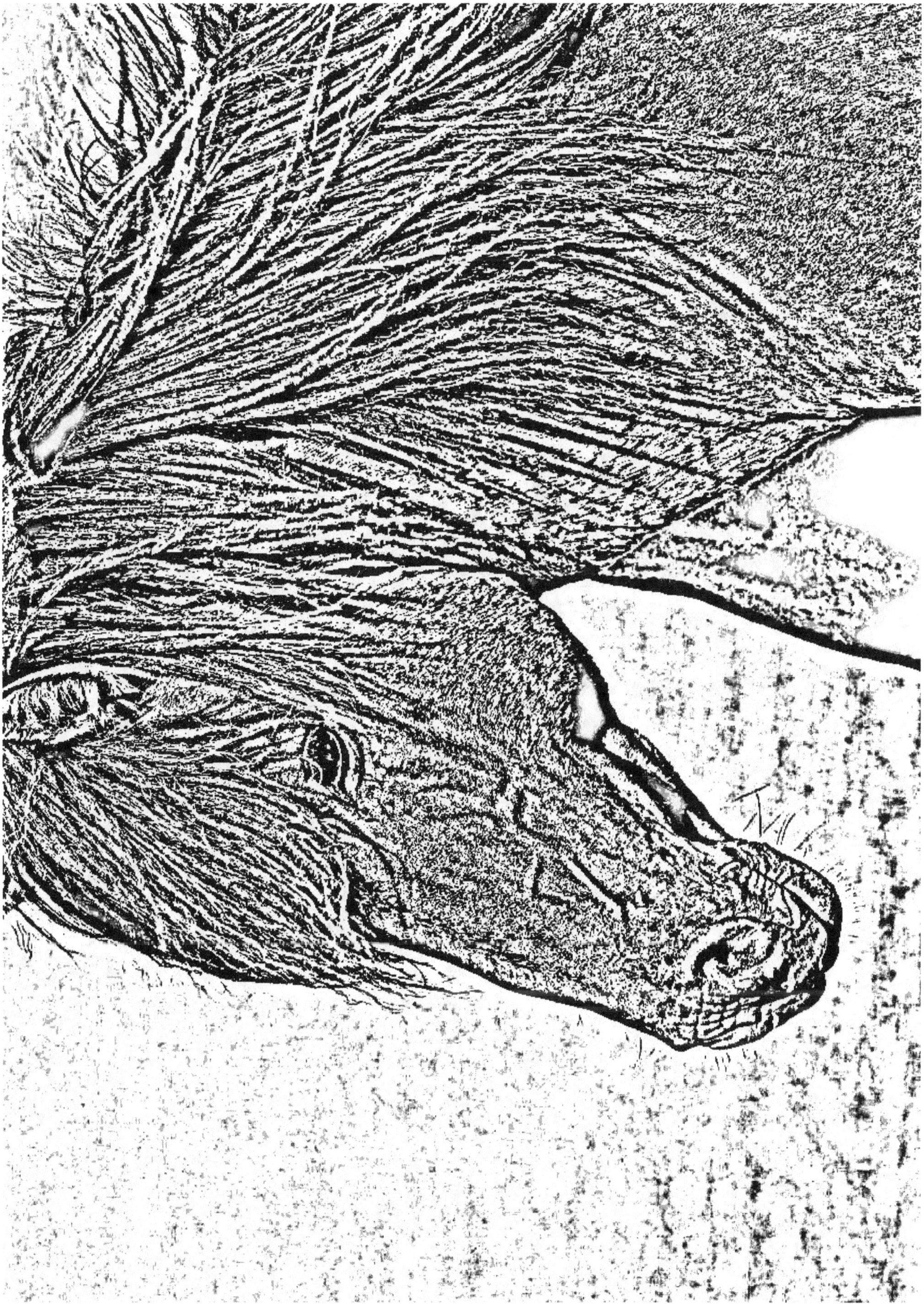

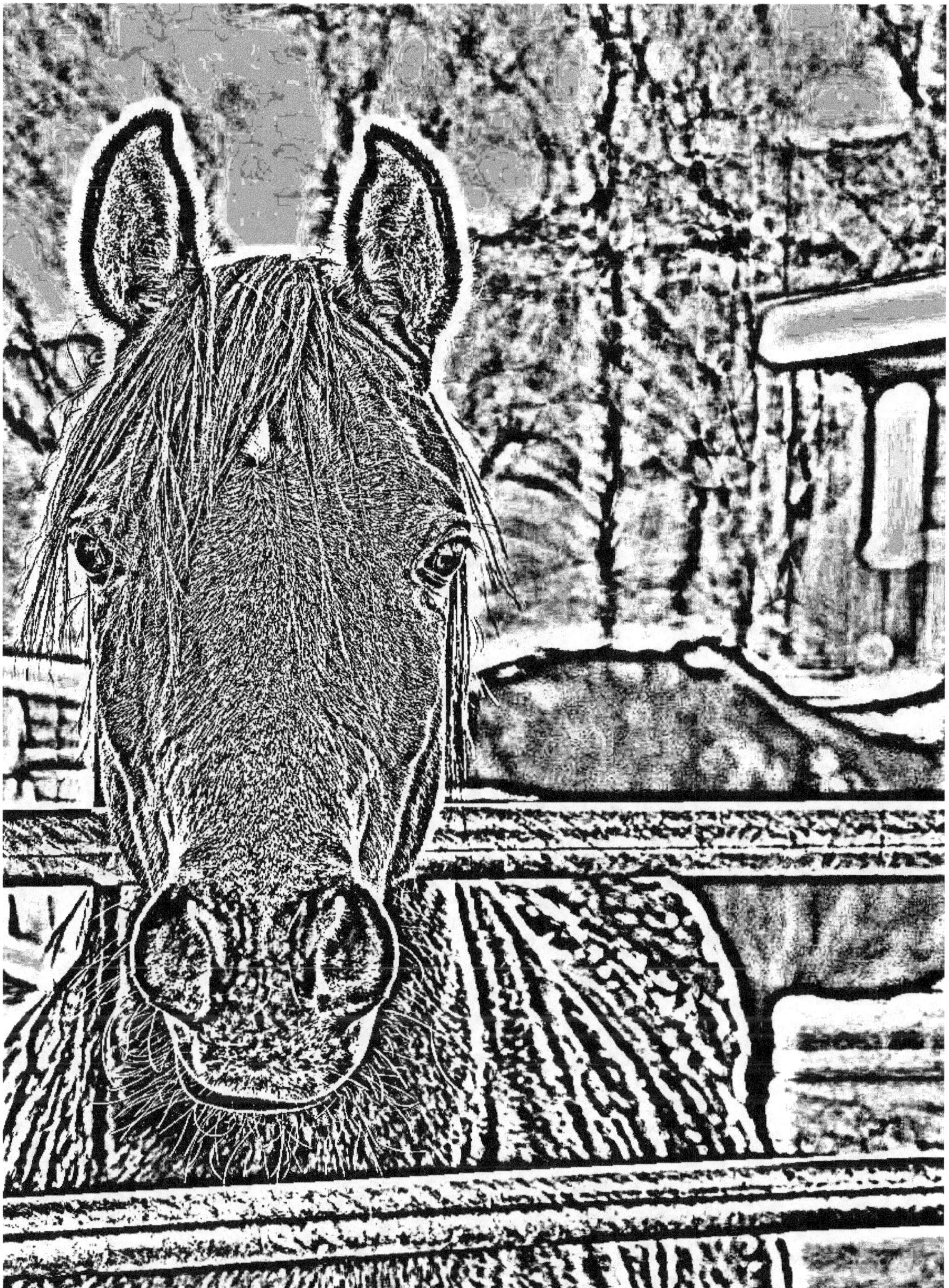

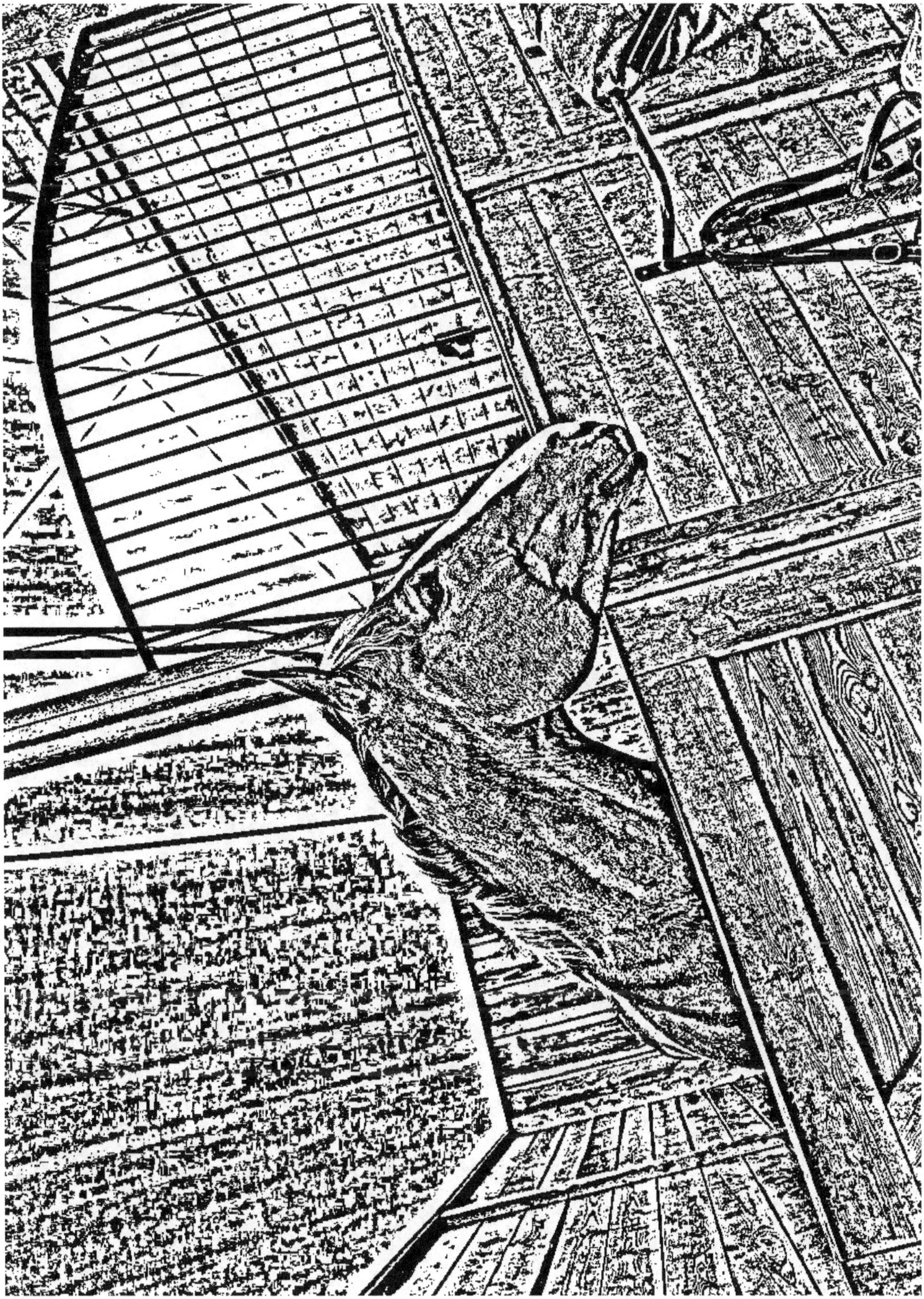

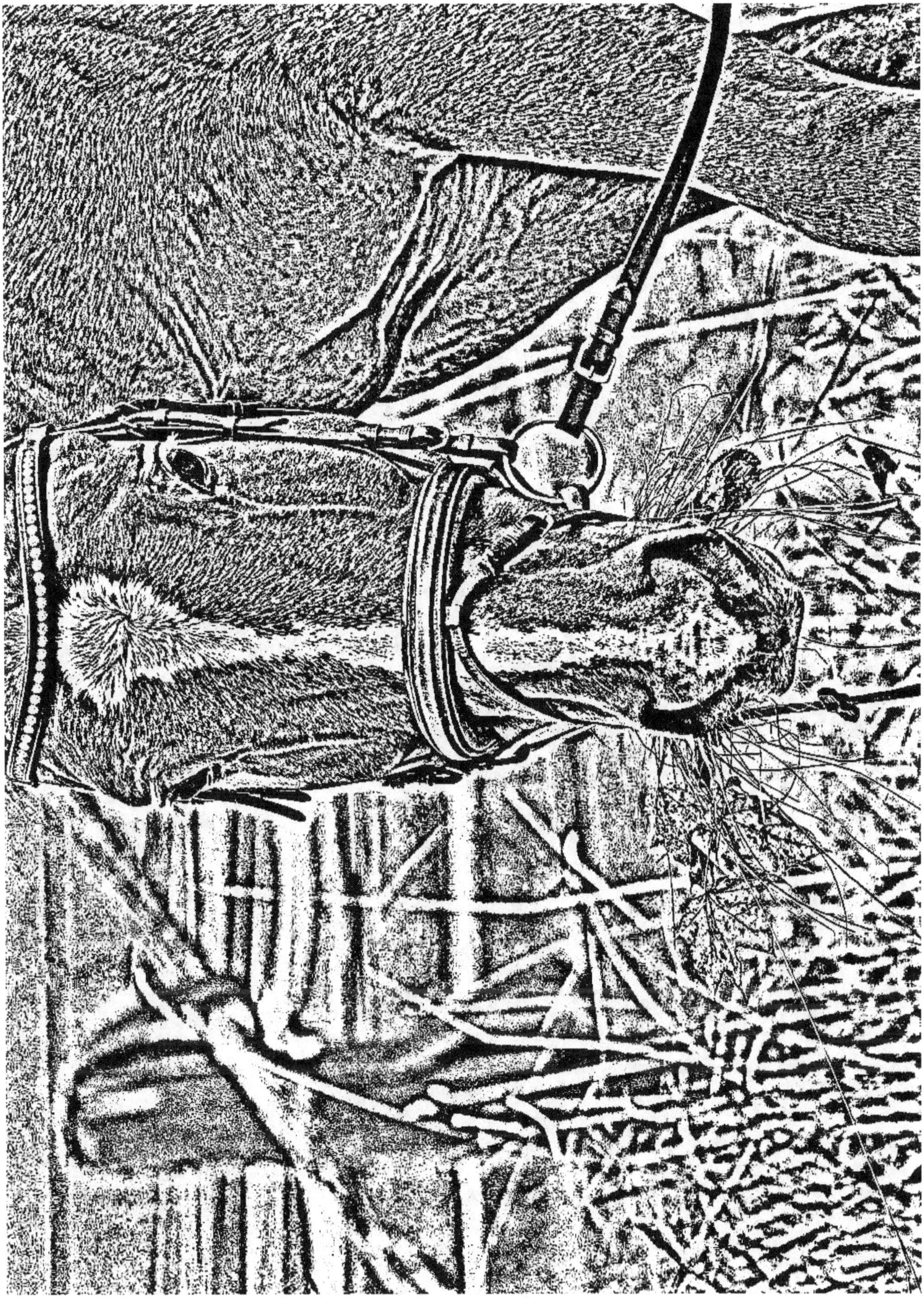

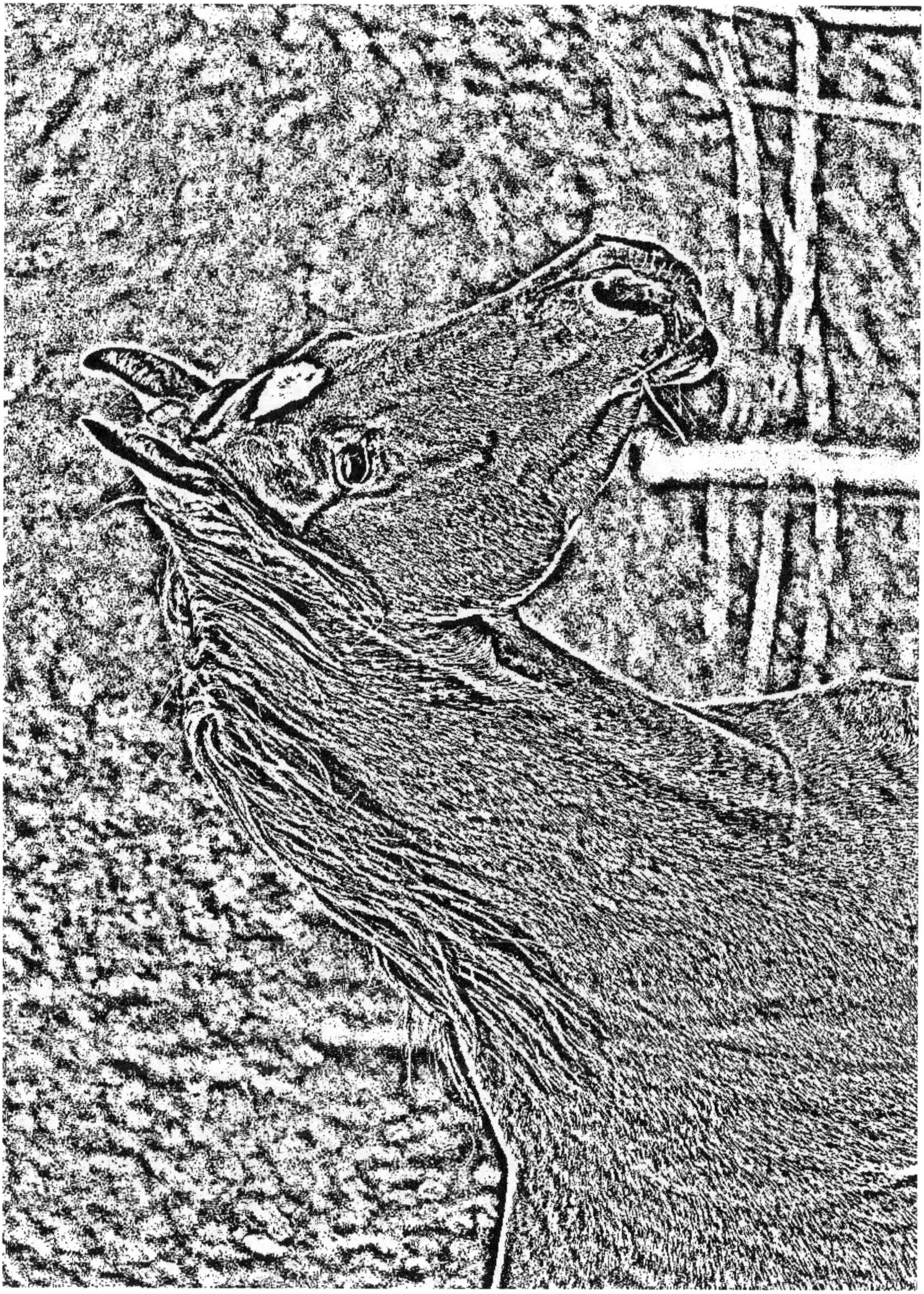

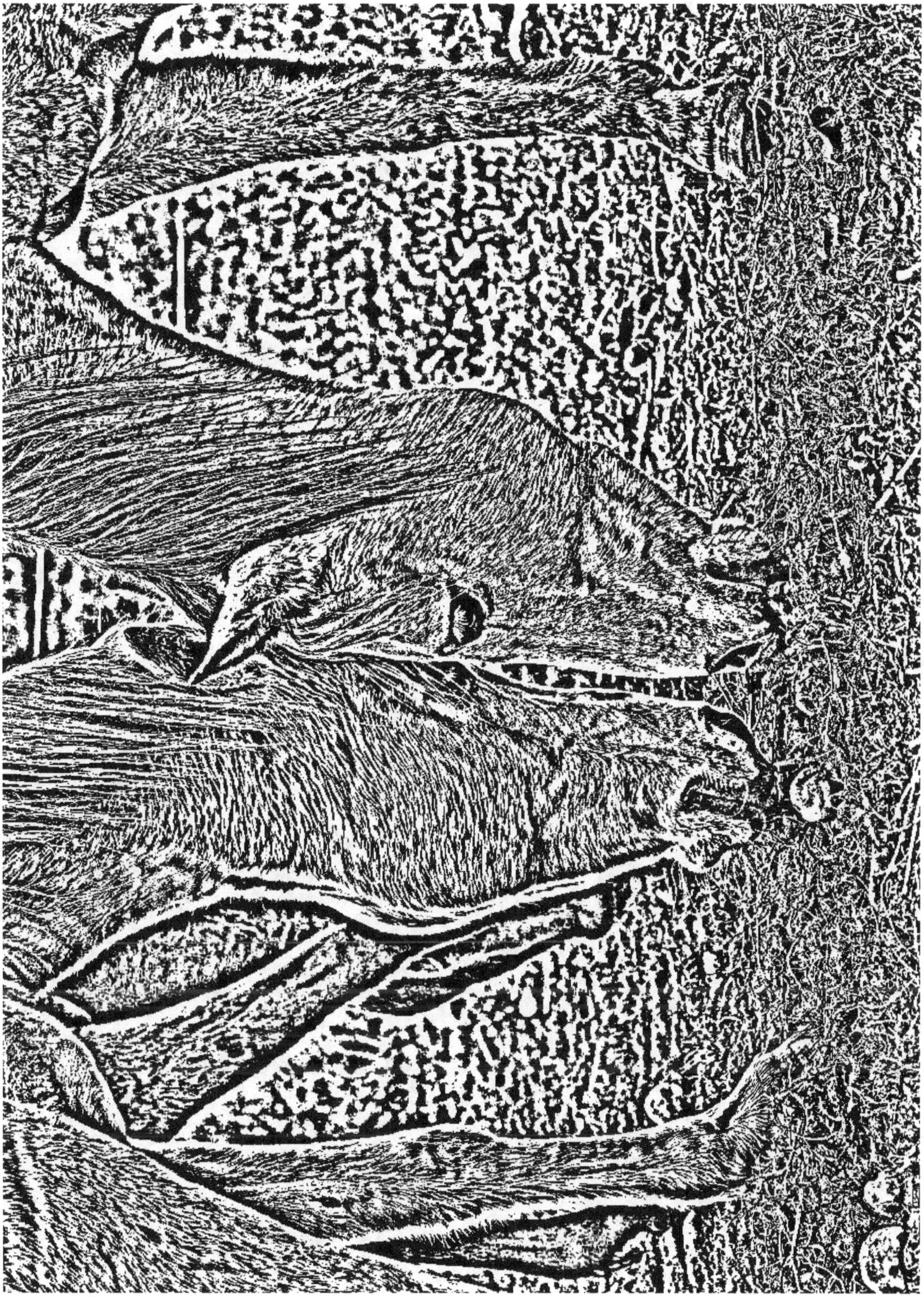

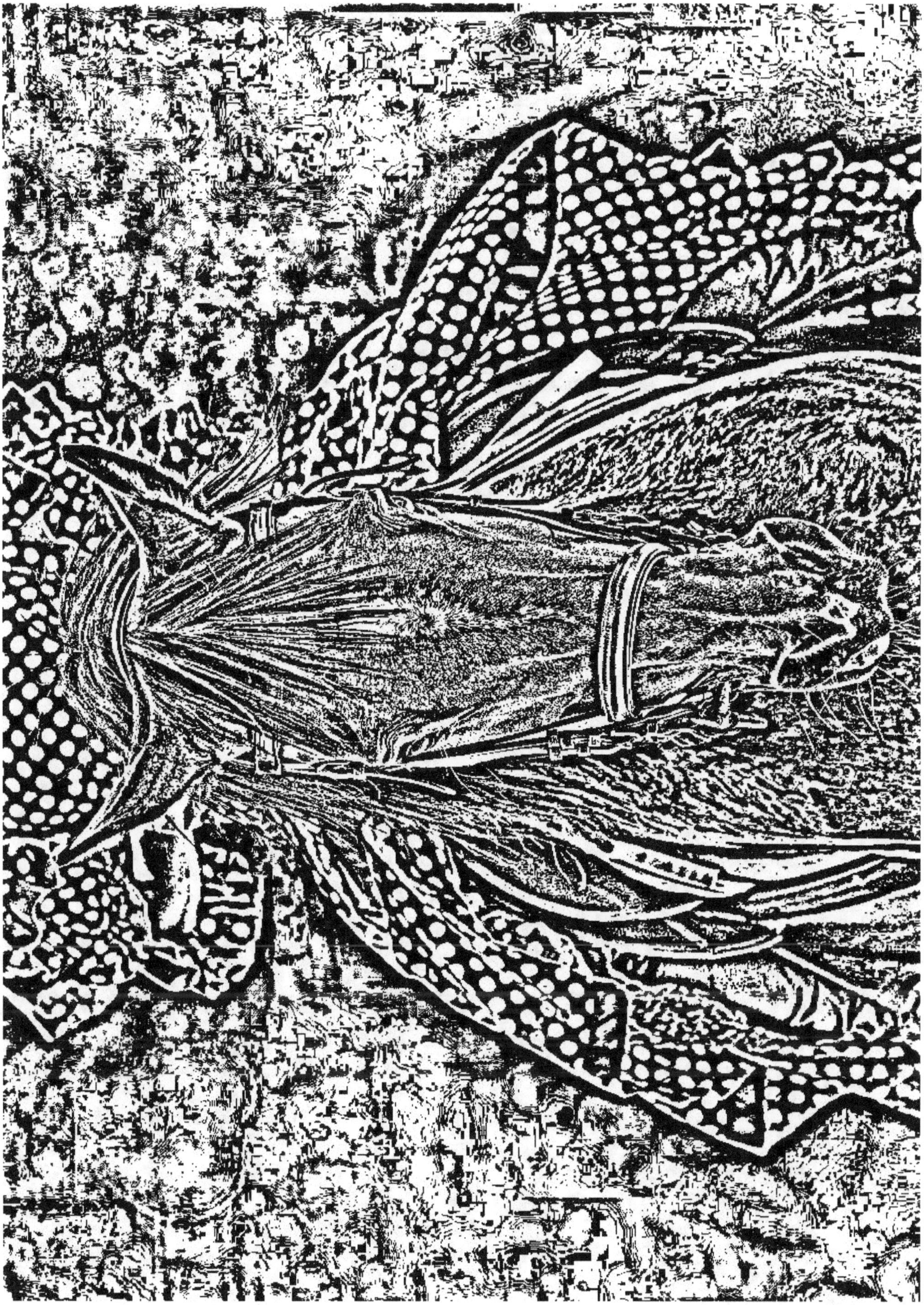

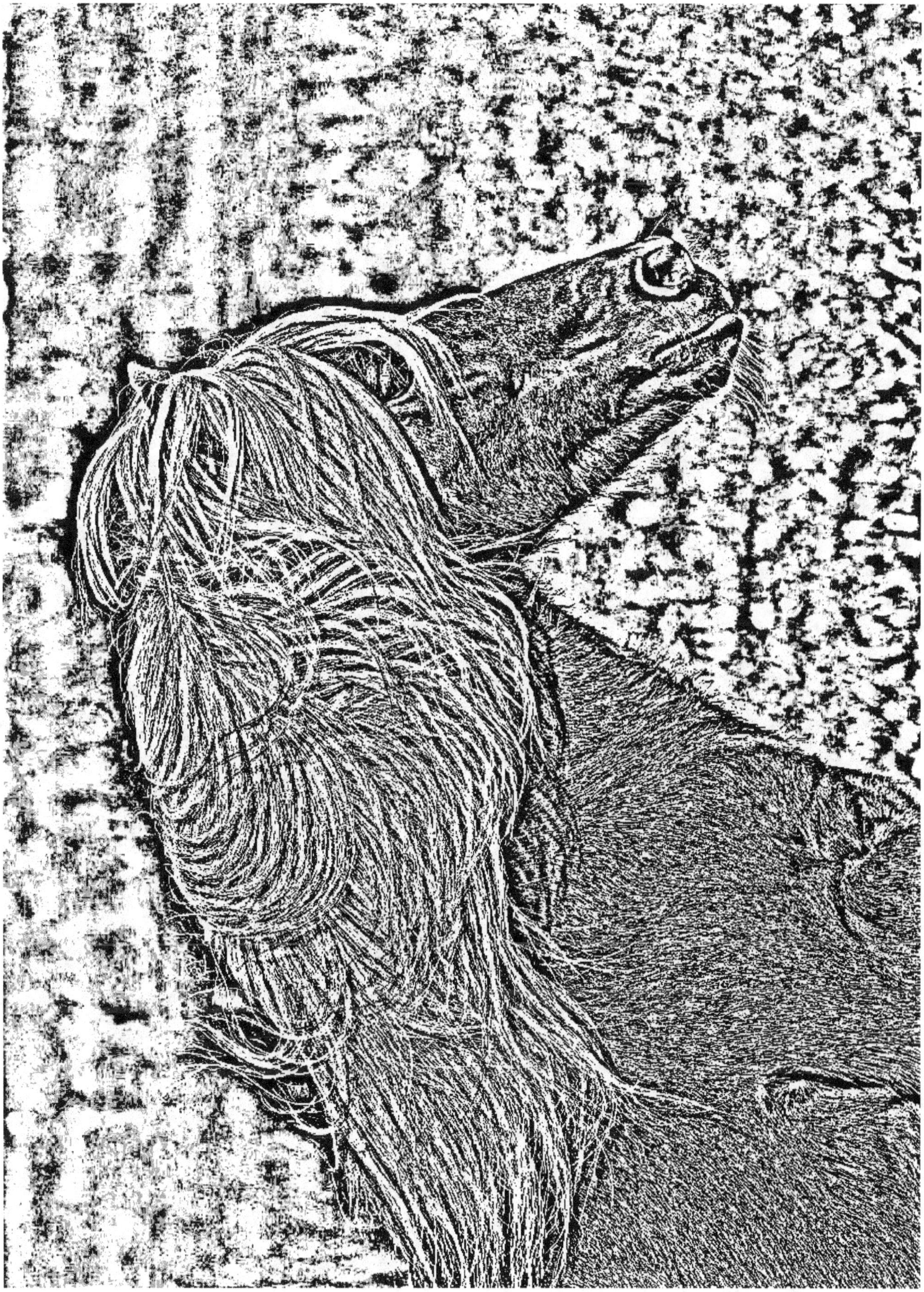

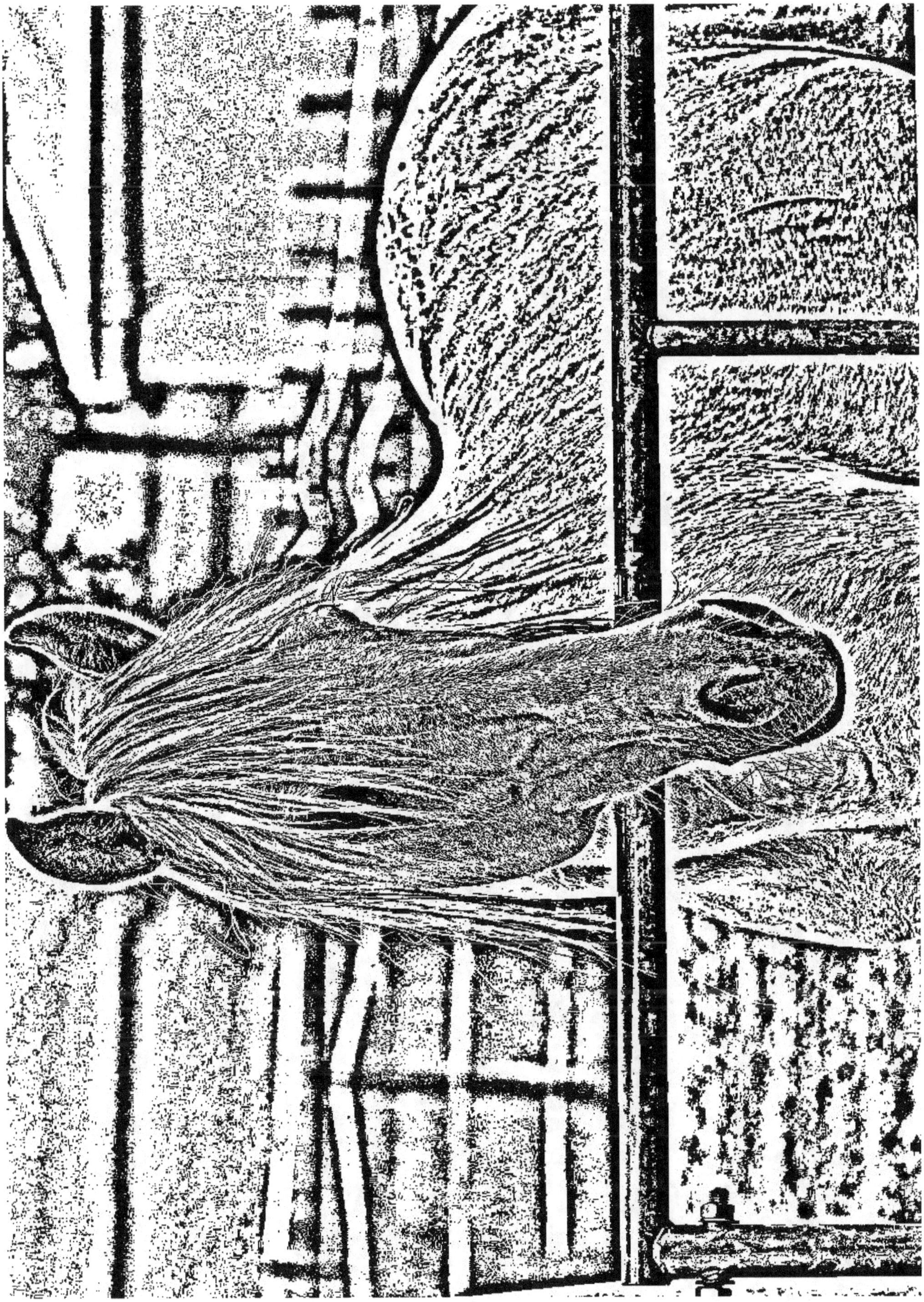

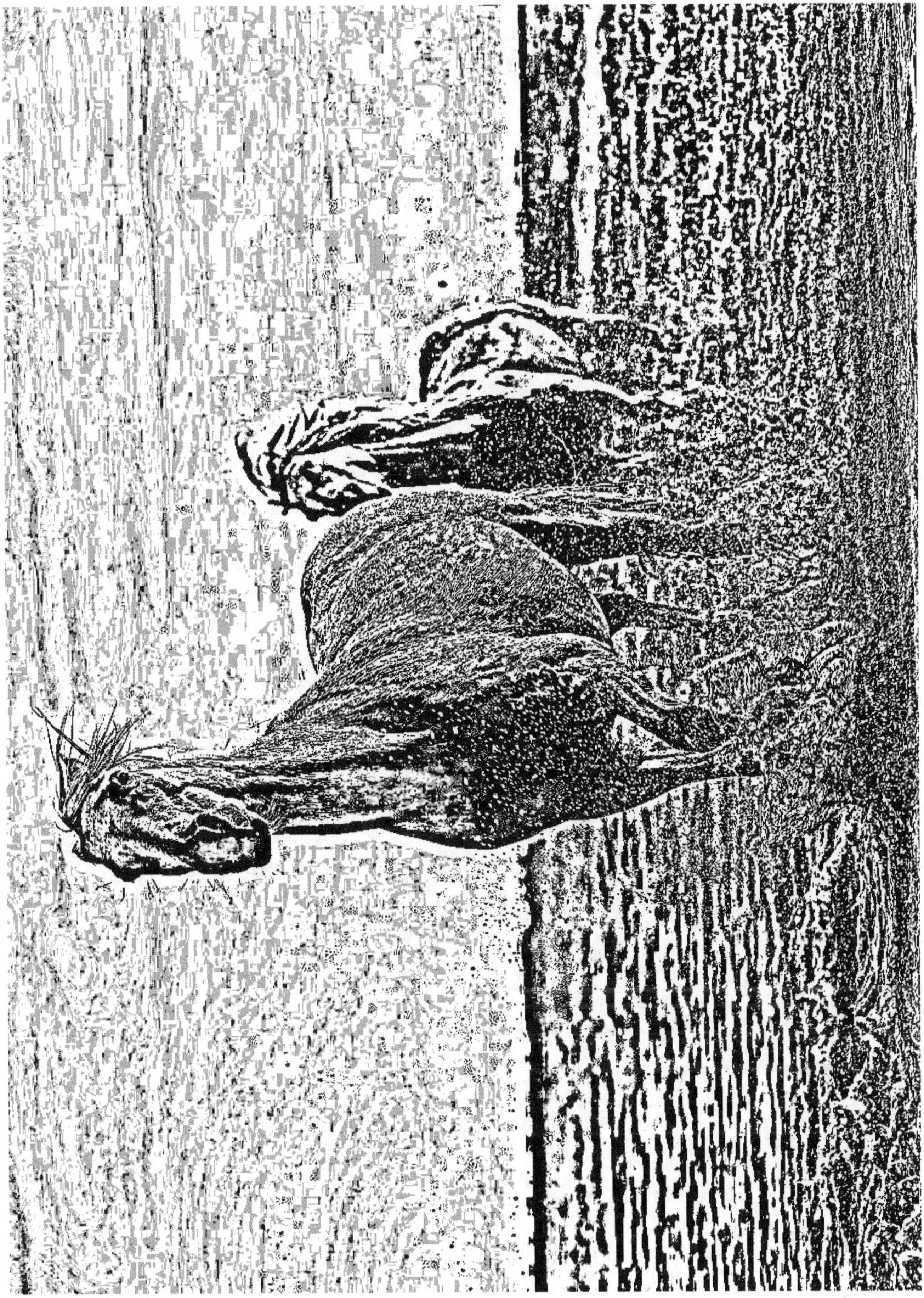

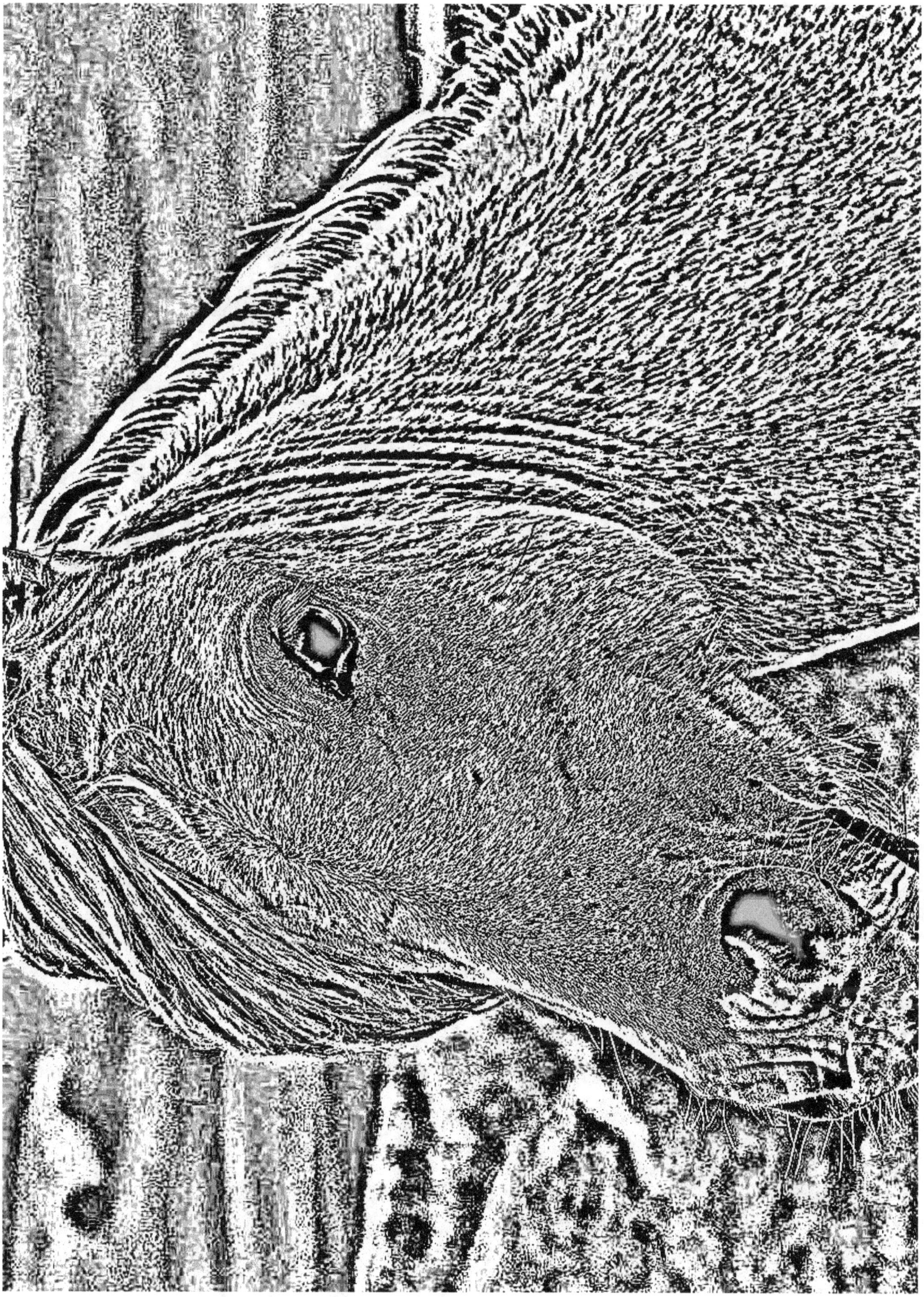

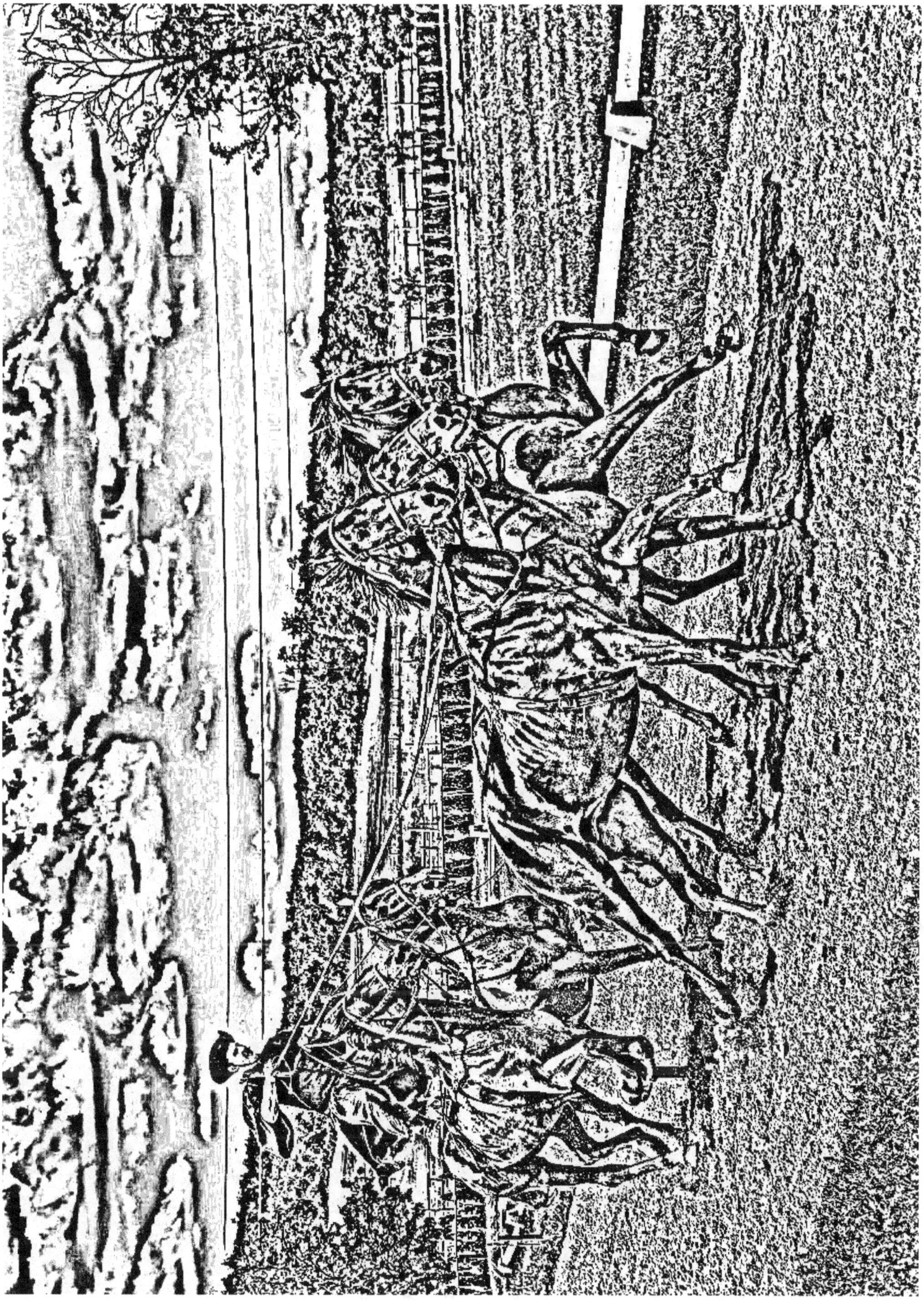

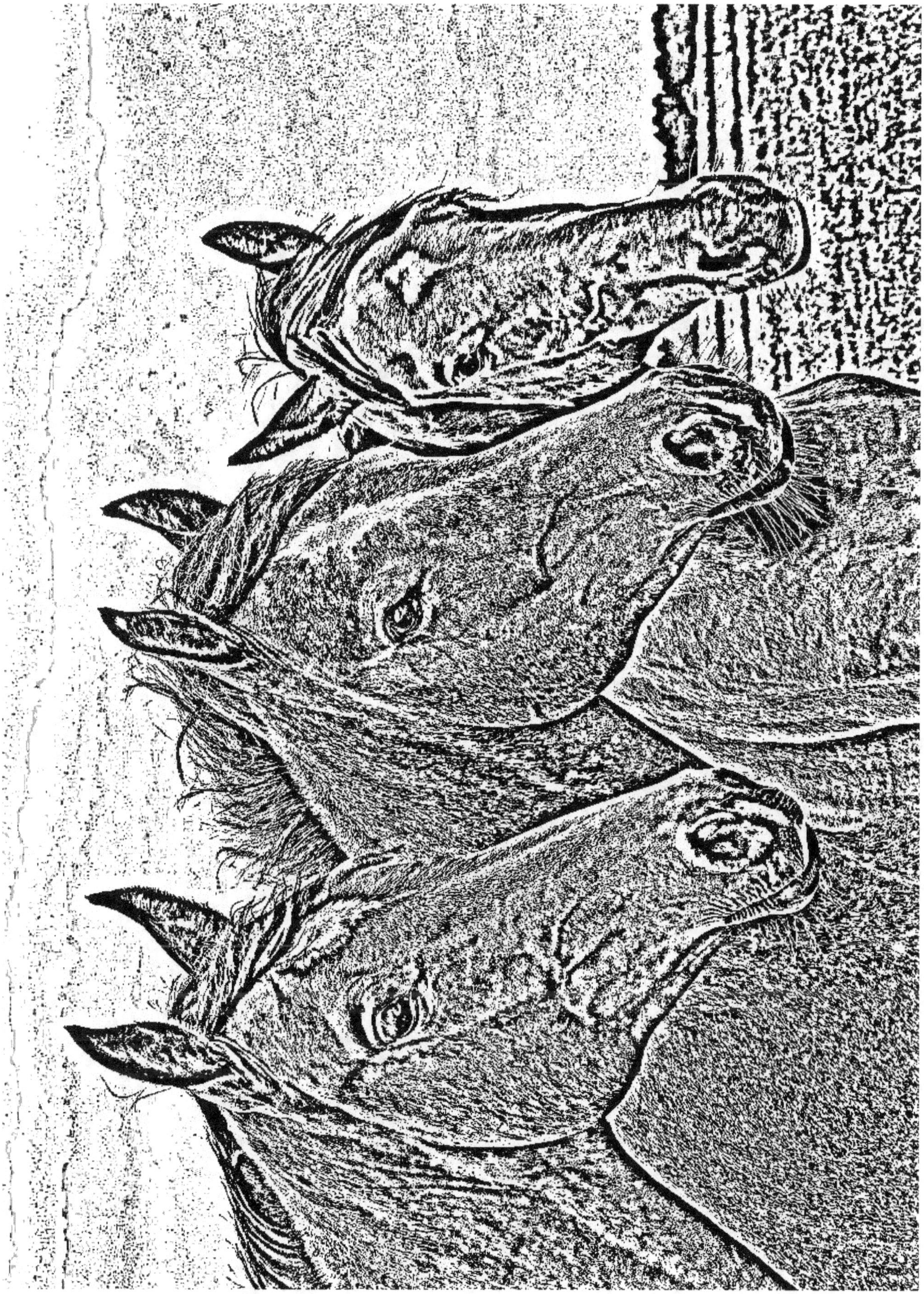

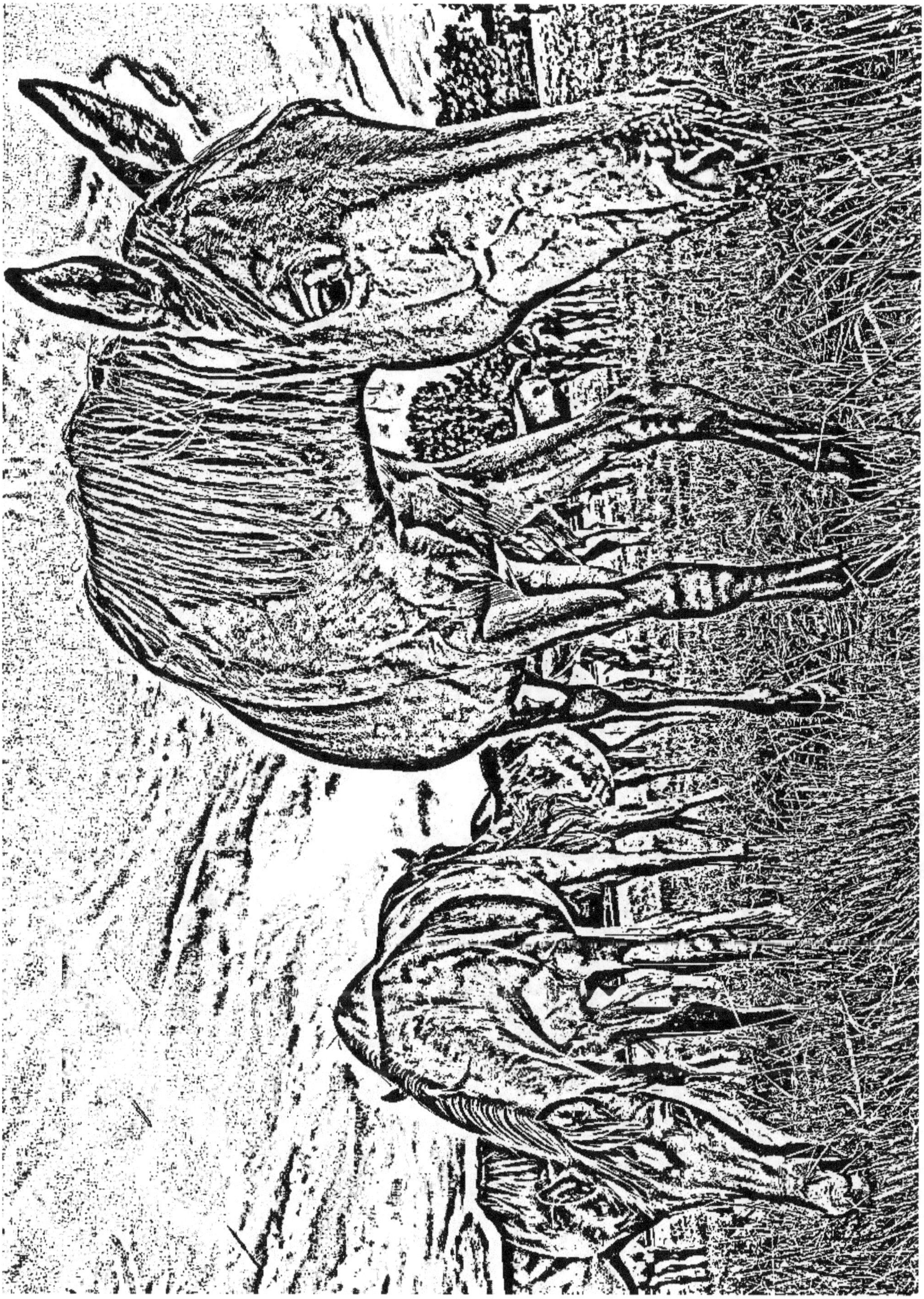

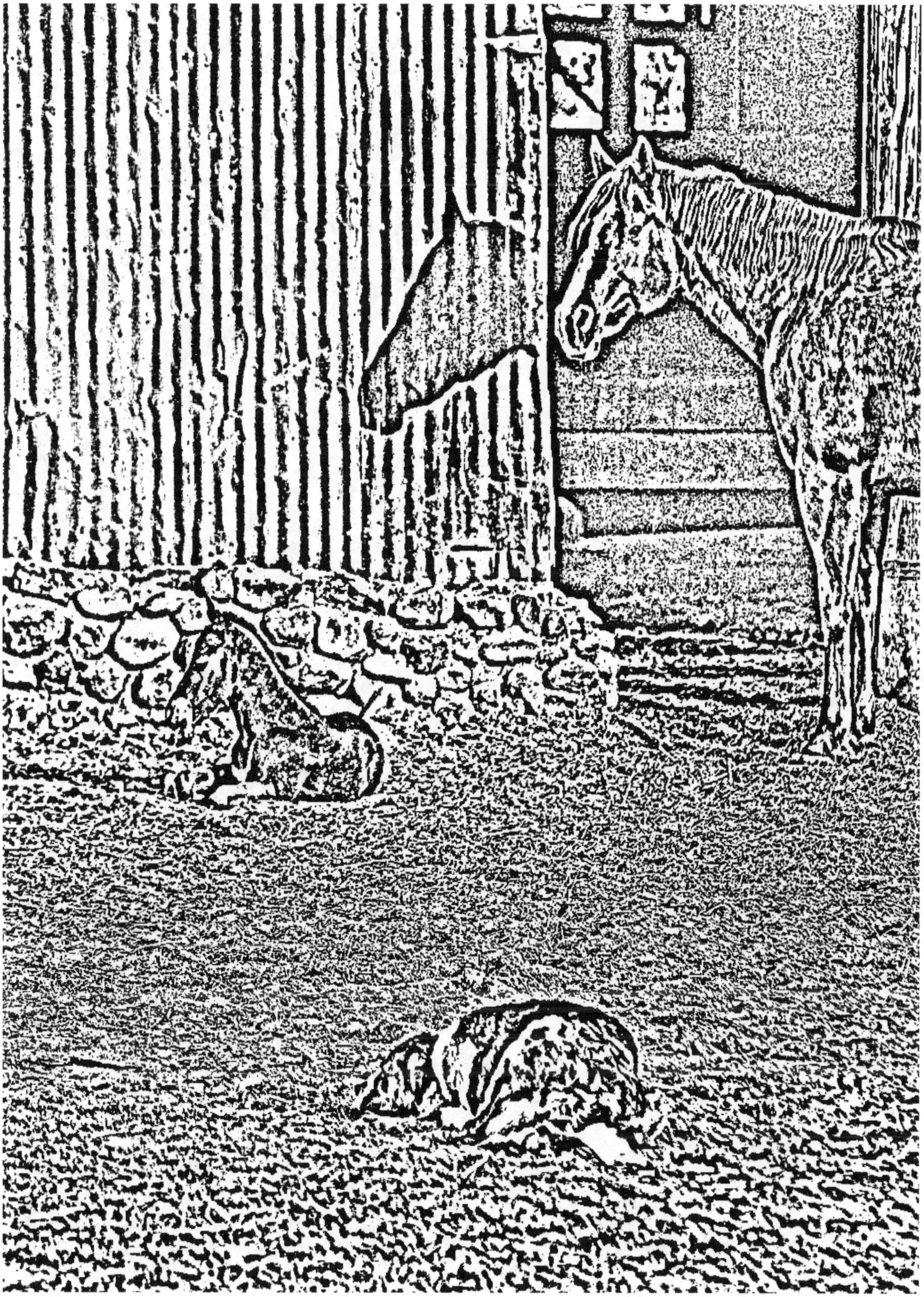

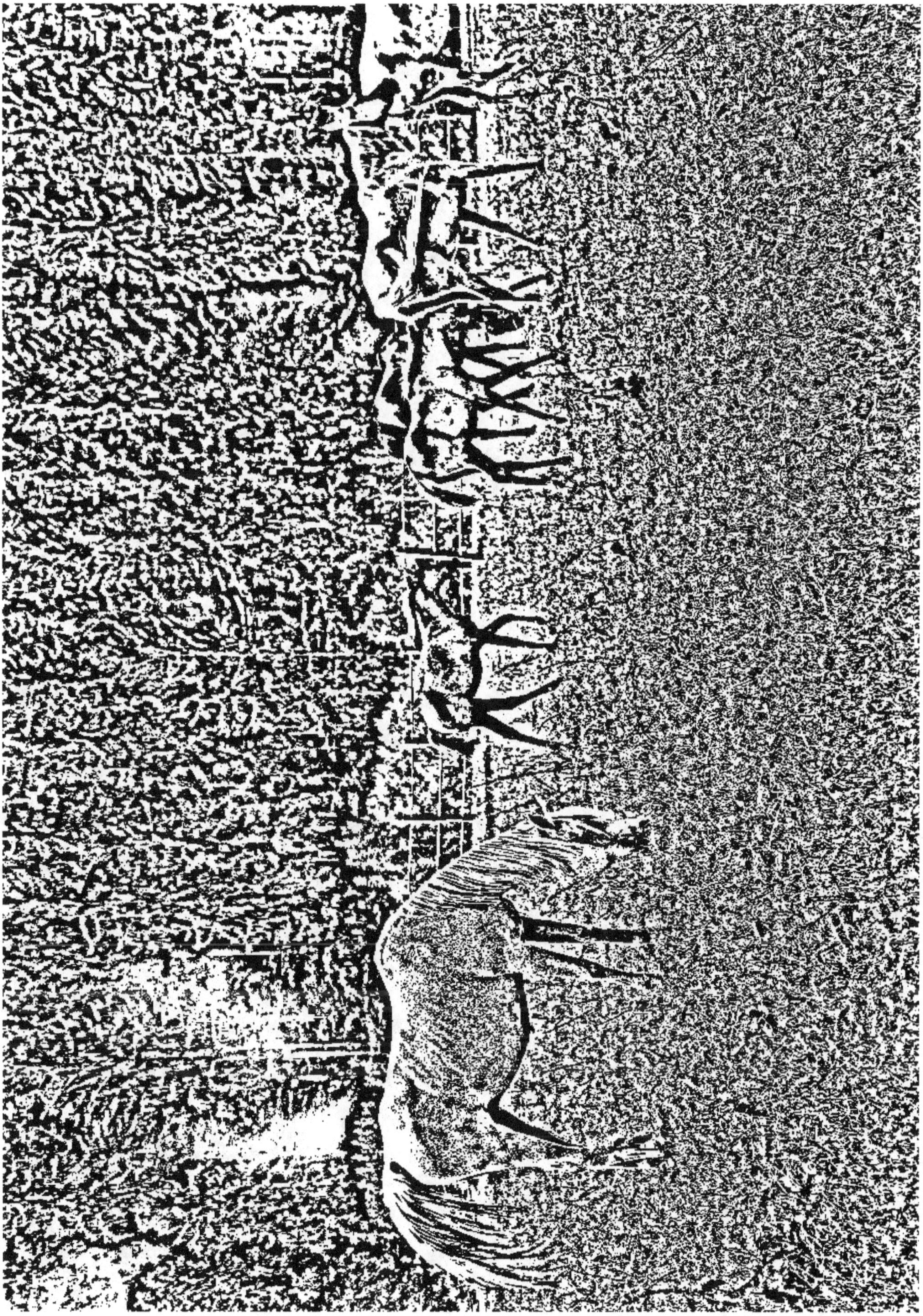

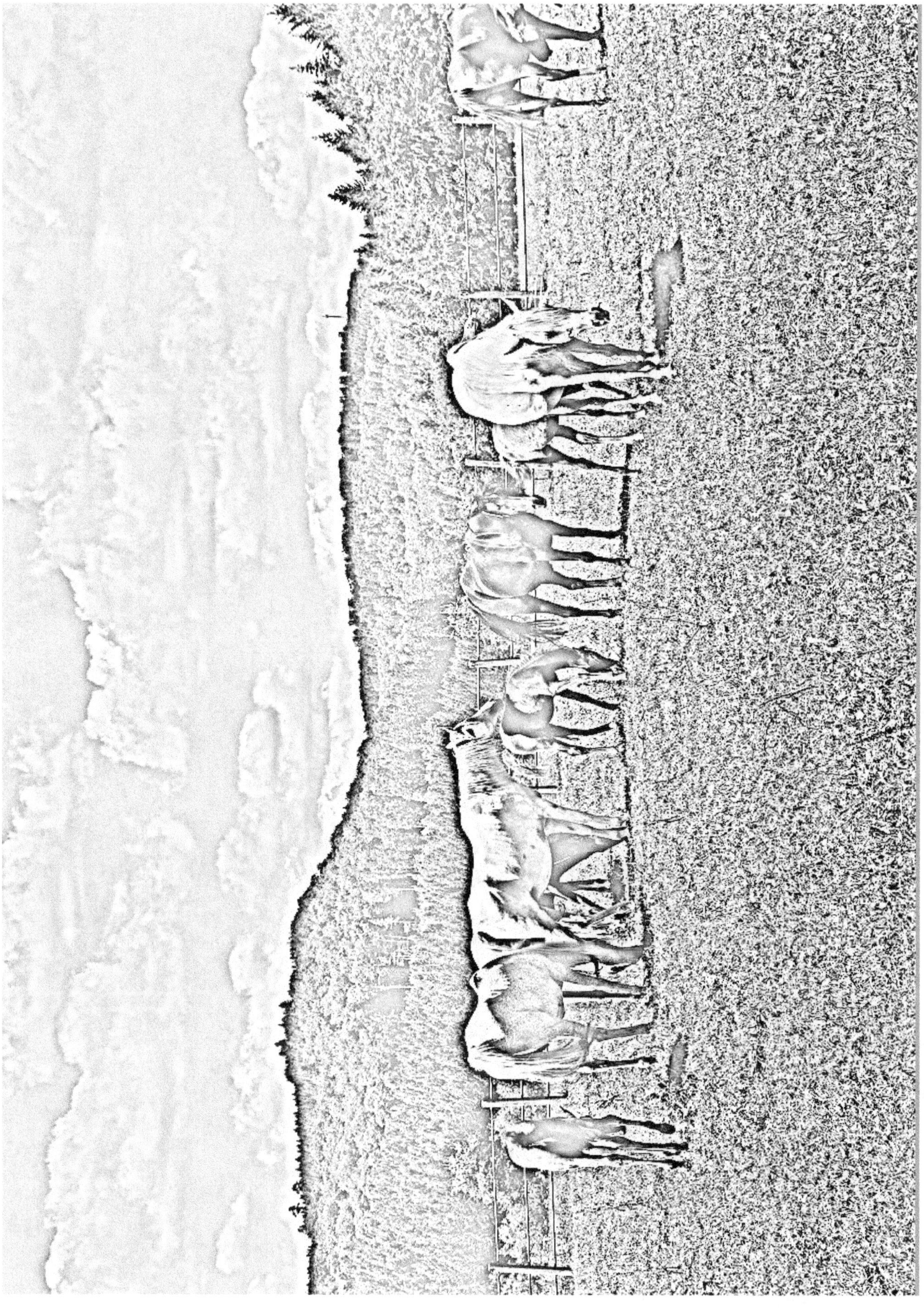

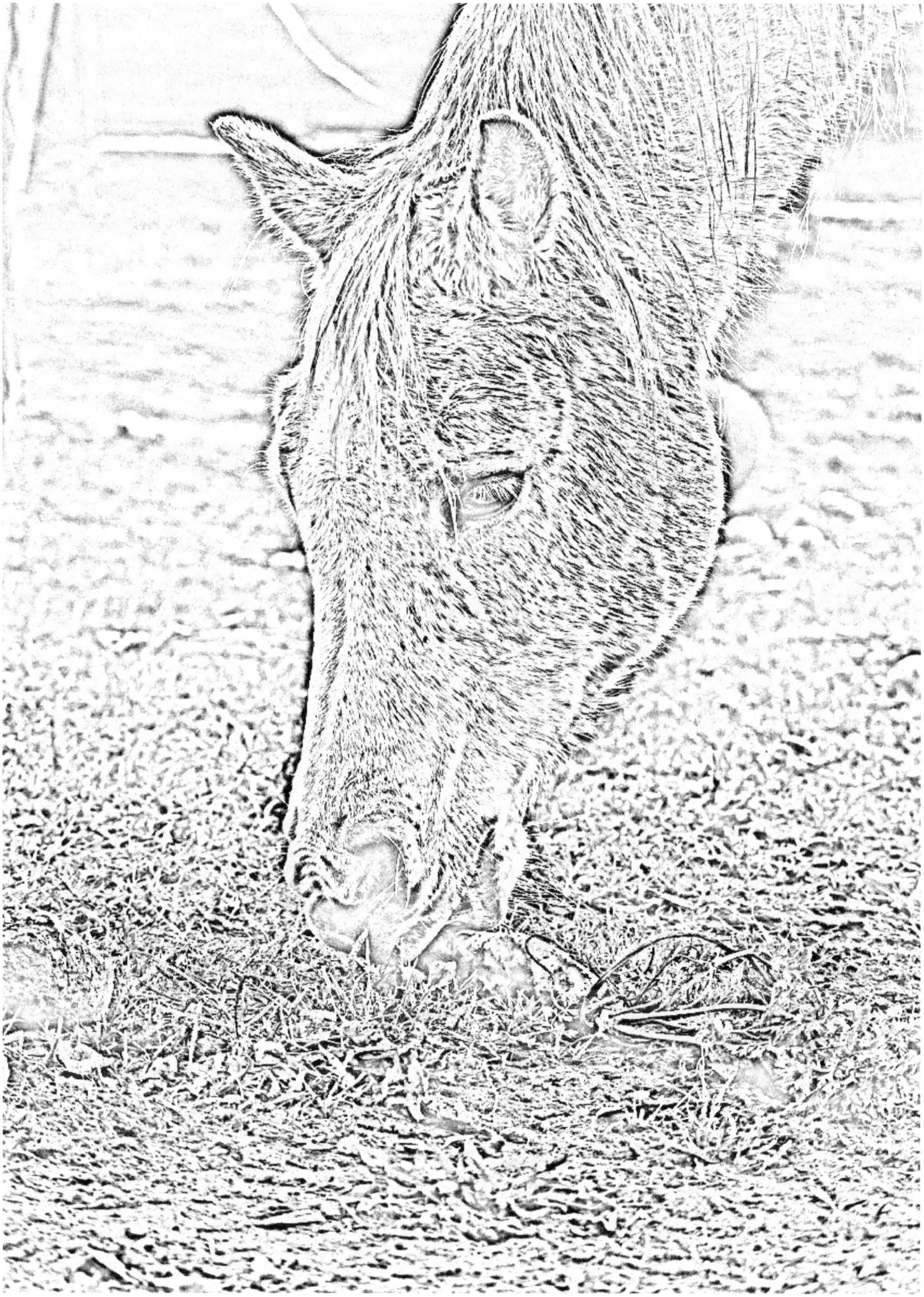

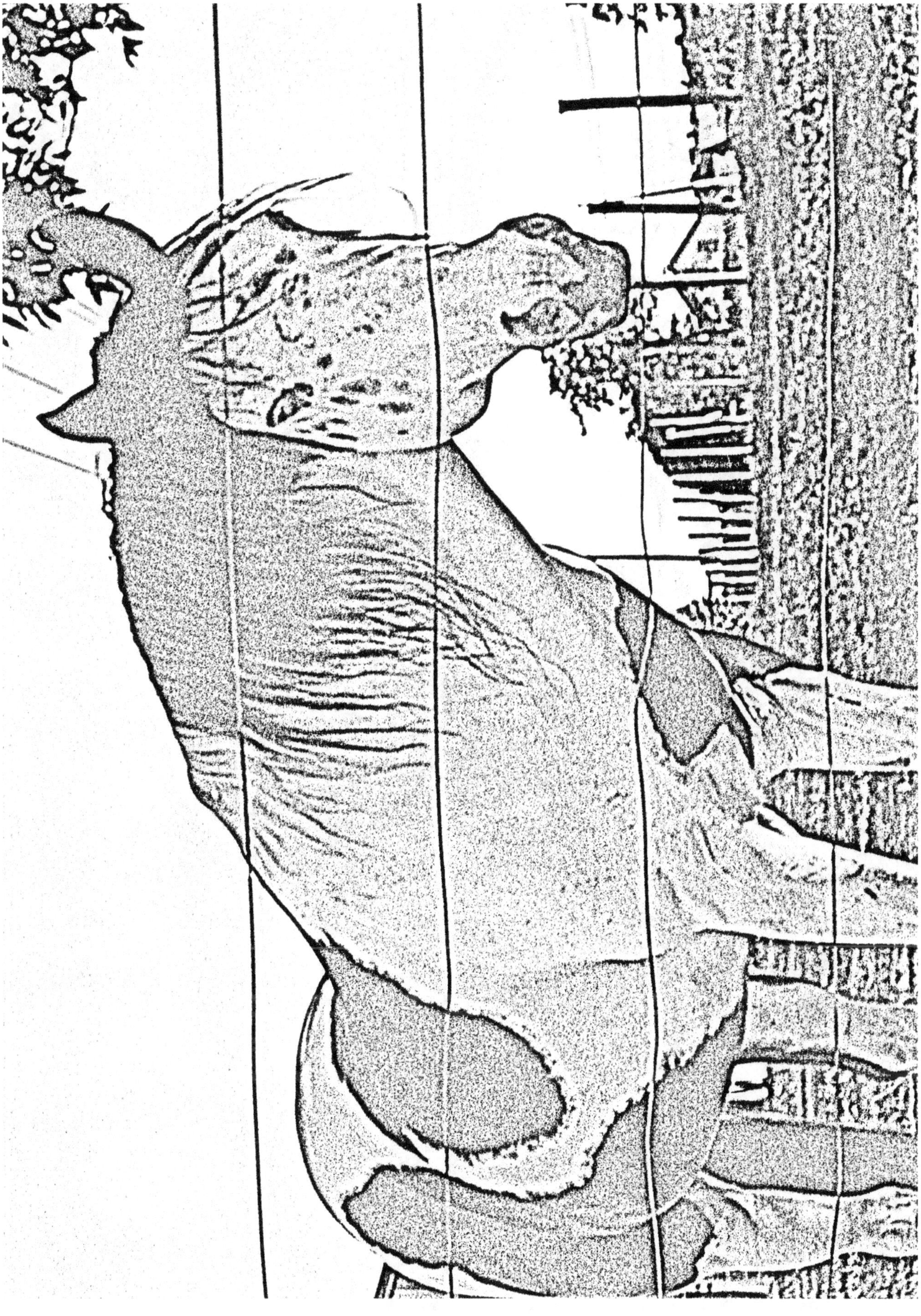

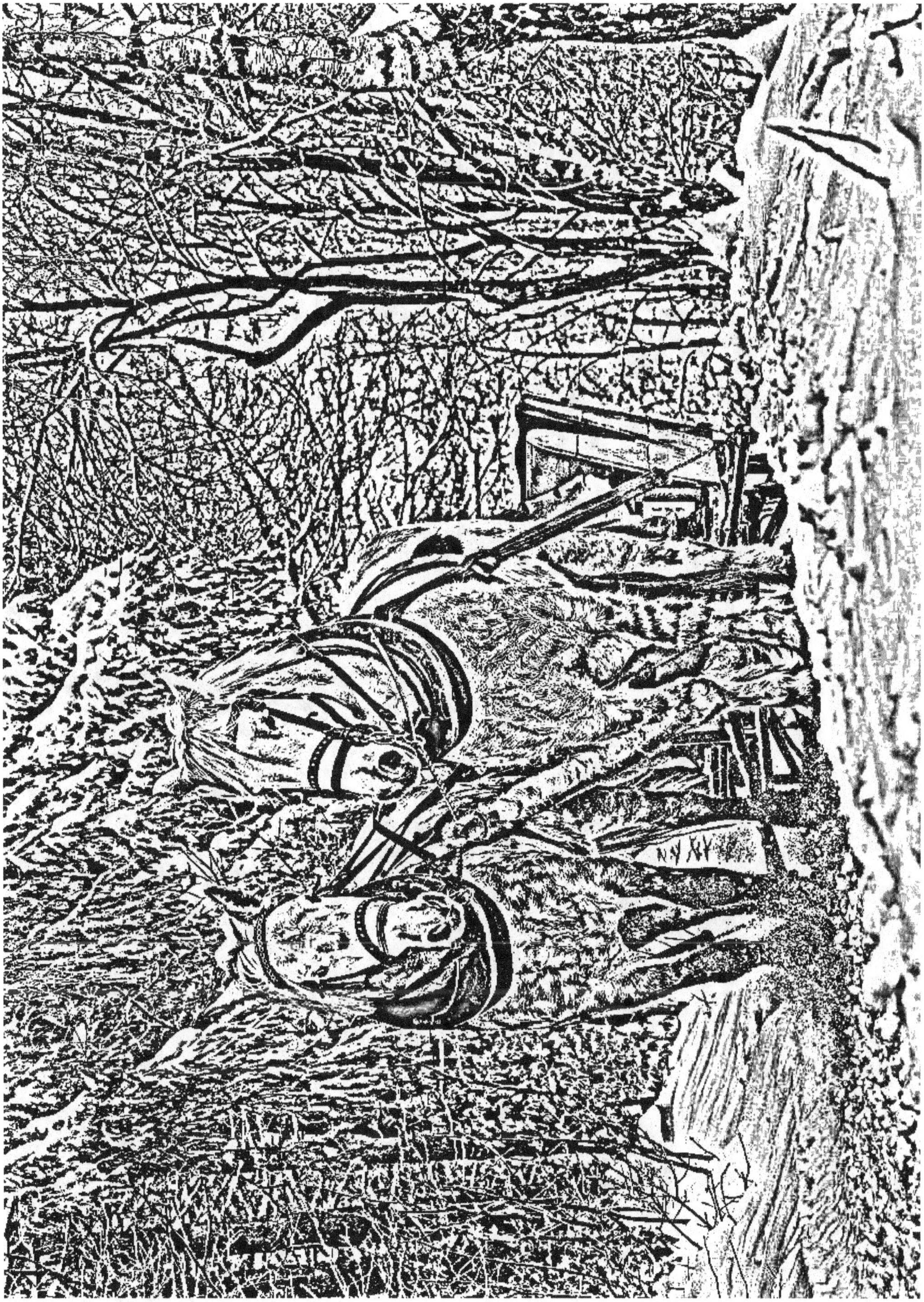

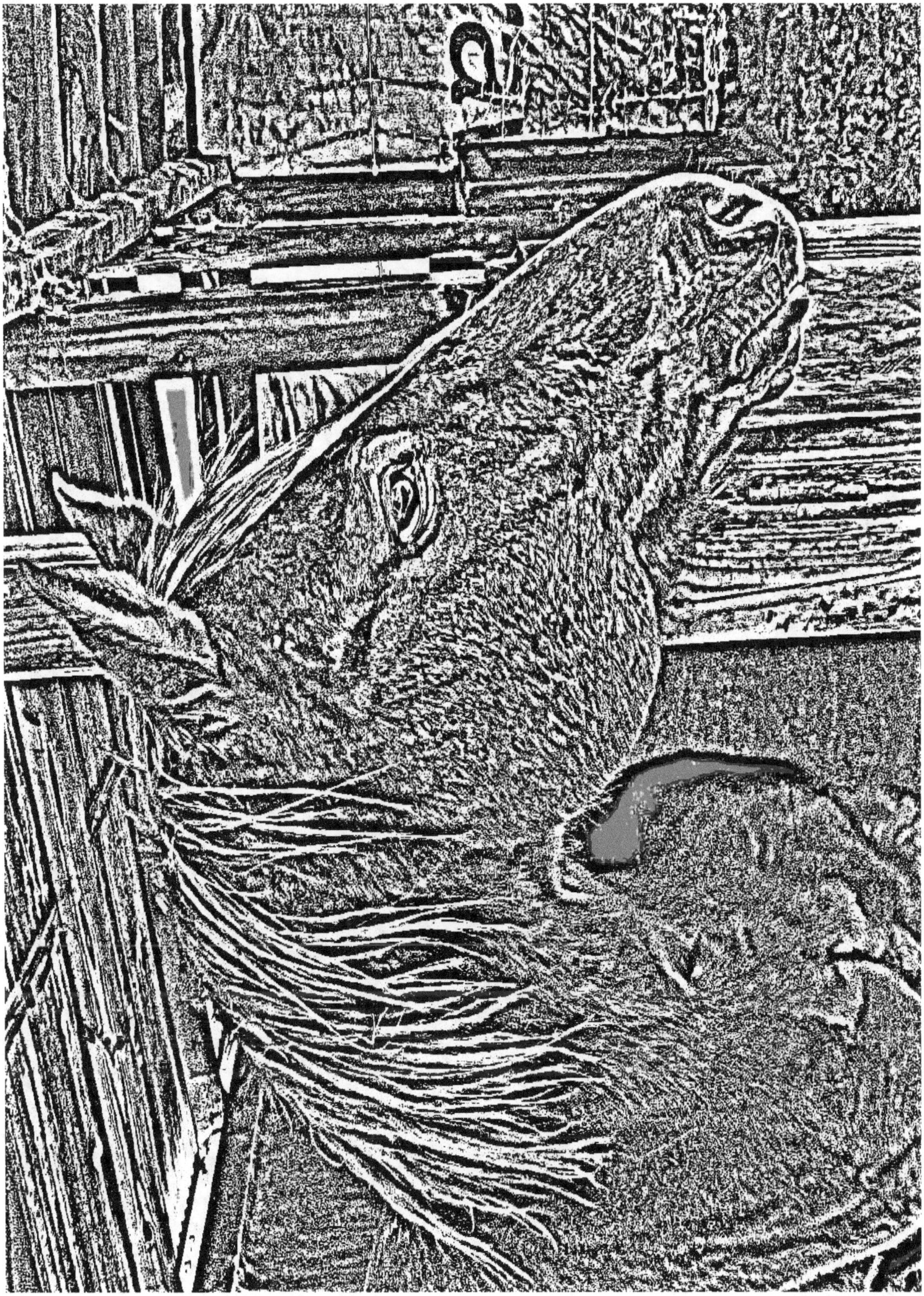

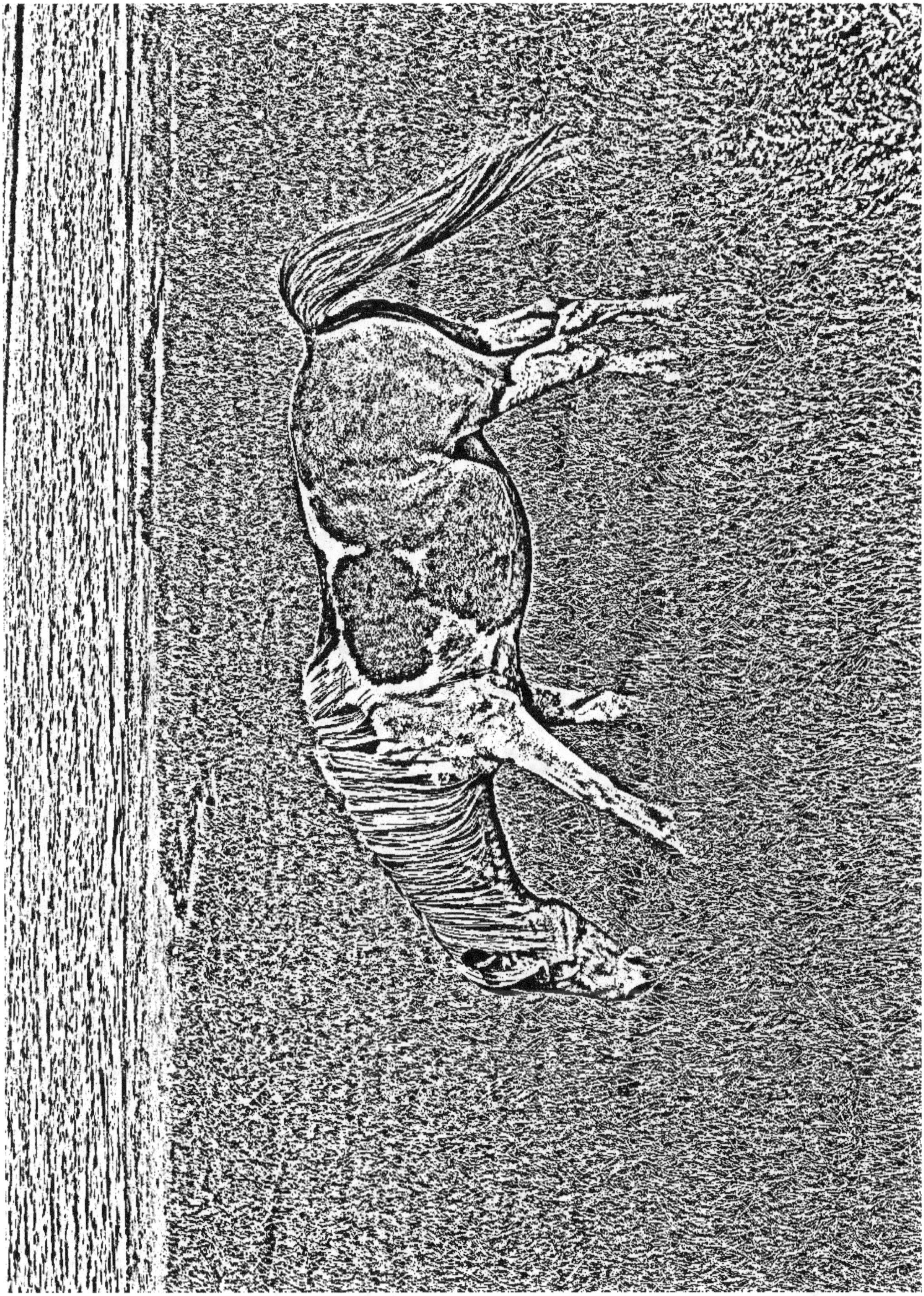

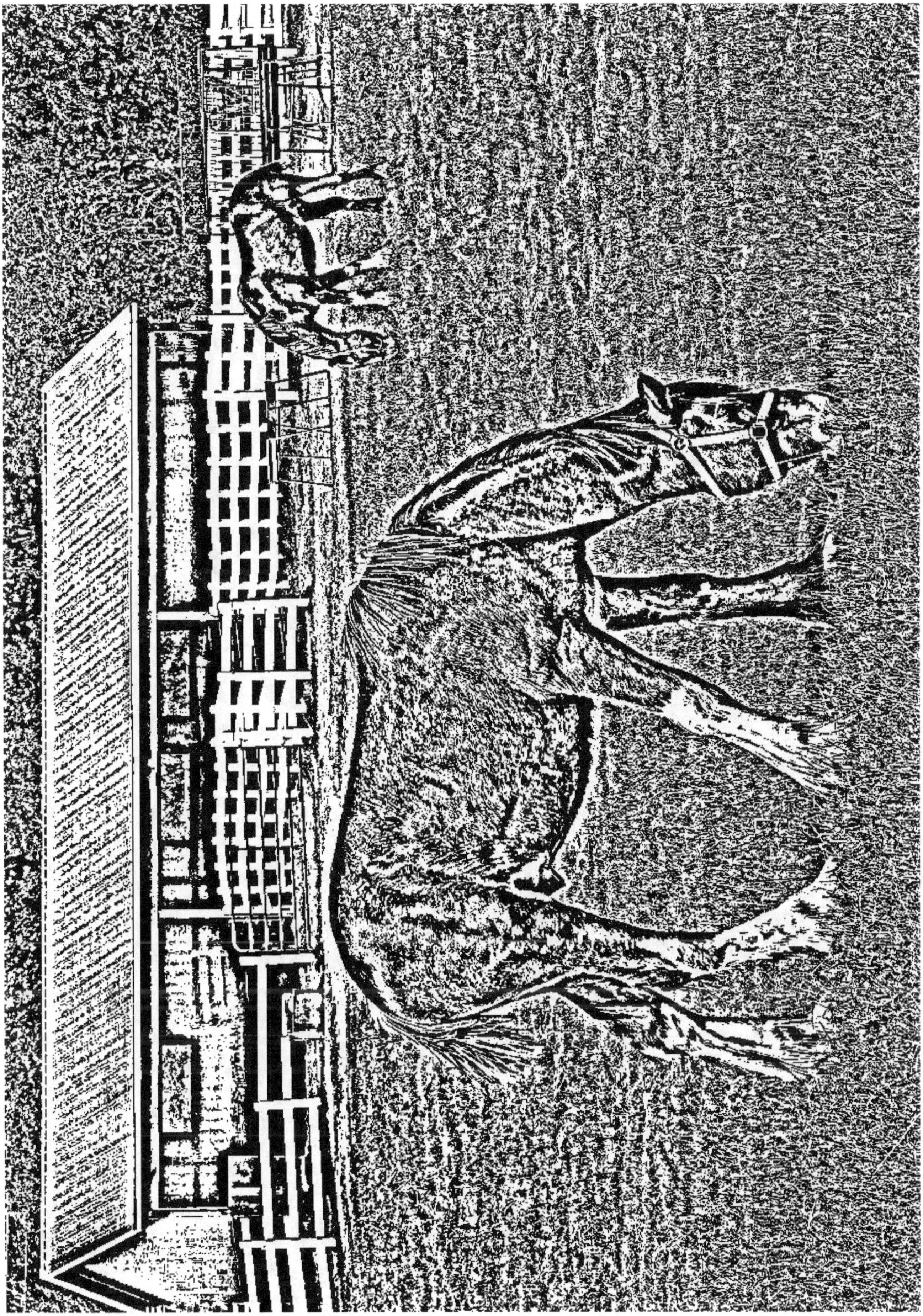

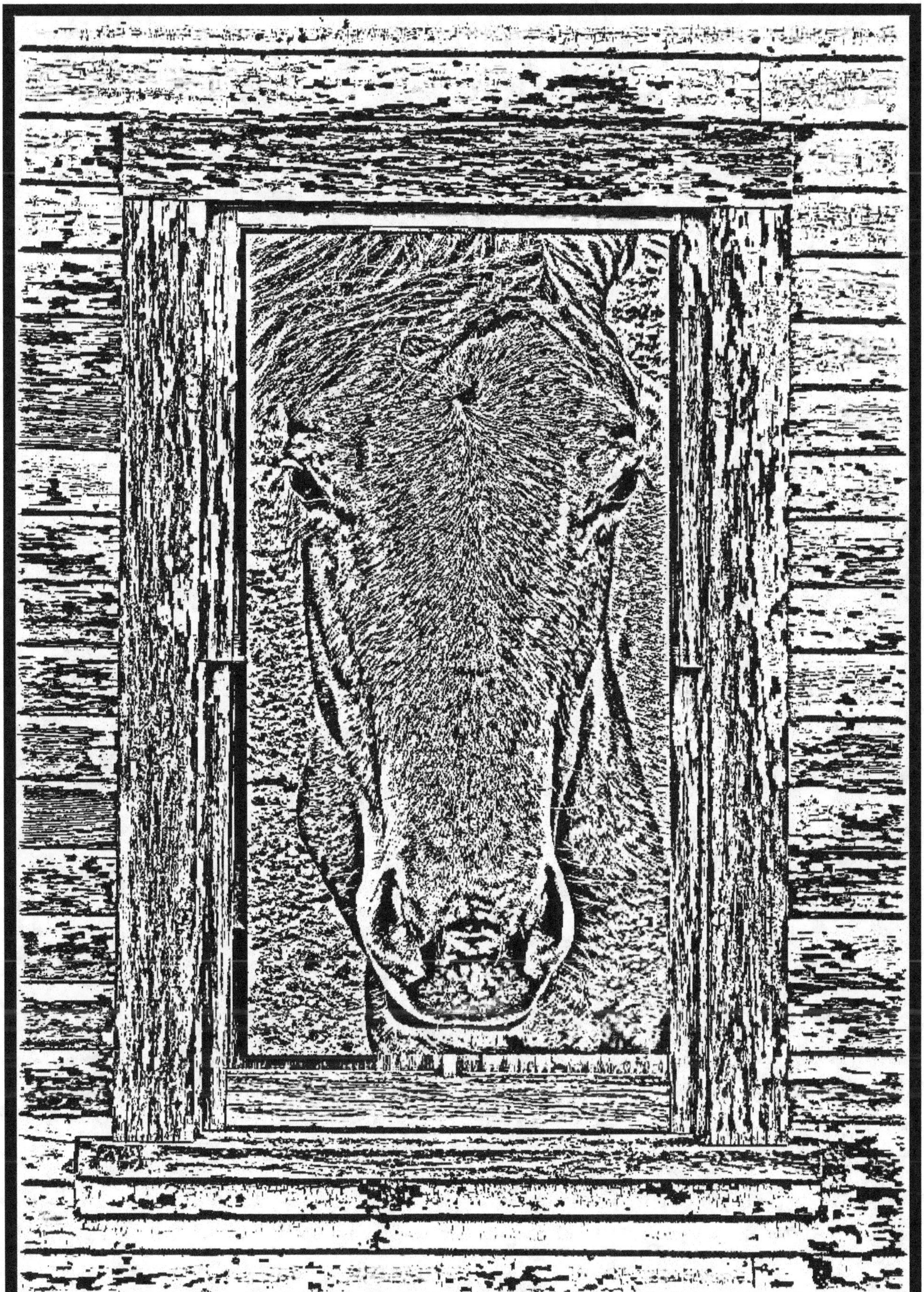

Thank you!
We hope you enjoyed our book.

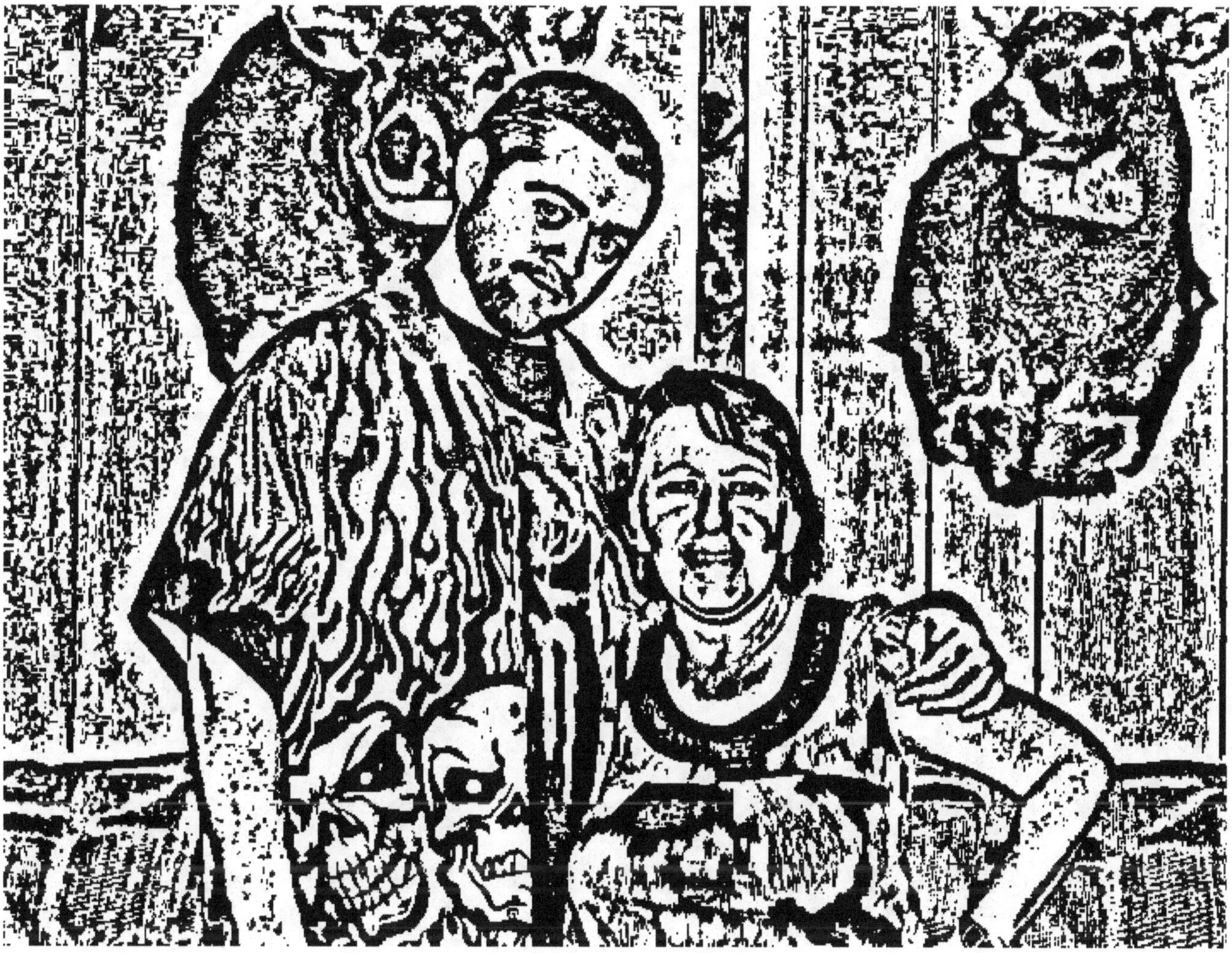

Watch for more color books by ARN Arts LLC.
Visit us at http://arnarts.wixsite.com/books.

www.ingramcontent.com/pod-product-compliance
Lightning Source LLC
Chambersburg PA
CBHW081124180526
45170CB00008B/2992
* 9 7 8 1 5 4 0 4 5 1 7 9 8 *